Bacchae

Euripides

Bacchae

Translated,
with an Introduction and Notes, by

Paul Woodruff

Hackett Publishing Company, Inc.
Indianapolis/Cambridge

Copyright © 1998 by Hackett Publishing Company, Inc.

05 04 03 02 01 00 99 98   1 2 3 4 5 6 7

For further information, please address
Hackett Publishing Company, Inc.
PO Box 44937
Indianapolis, IN 46244-0937

Cover design by Brian Rak and John Pershing
Text design by Meera Dash

Library of Congress Cataloging-in-Publication Data

Euripides.
    [Bacchae. English]
    Bacchae / Euripides : translated, with introduction and notes, by
Paul Woodruff.
        p.   cm.
    Includes bibliographical references (p.   ).
    ISBN 0-87220-392-1 (paper : alk. paper). — ISBN 0-87220-393-X
(cloth : alk. paper)
    1. Dionysus (Greek deity)—Drama. 2. Pentheus (Greek mythology—
Drama. 3. Bacchantes—Drama. I. Woodruff, Paul, 1943–   .
II. Title.
PA3975.B2W66   1999
882'.01—dc21   98-37826
                                                                    CIP

The paper used in this publication meets the minimum requirements of
American National Standard for Information Sciences—Permanence of
Paper for Printed Library Materials, ANSI Z39.48-1984.
                                    ∞

Contents

Translator's Preface

This translation is intended primarily for classroom use. I have aimed first of all at being clear and true to the basic meaning of the text. After that, I have tried to bring across some of the beauty of poetry given the chorus as well as the rhetorical power and cleverness of the dialogue and speeches. And I have tried to give the characters the different voices I hear in the Greek, so that the translation can be produced on stage with minimal changes.

The transmission of this play through manuscripts is unusually troublesome; many lines seem to have fallen out during copying and storage over the centuries and many errors have been introduced. Although I have supplied a few lines to fill small gaps where the meaning is obvious, I have not devised speeches to make up for the lost passages at the end; instead, I have included an appendix with the main evidence we have that pertains to them. In a stage production, I would have the messenger declare that the speeches are lost and summarize their content.

In the cult songs and other lyric passages given to the chorus, I have tried to preserve their concision, their striking use of compound formations, and their ambiguities. I have avoided the repetitions with which some translators have tried to render poetic and religious elements.

The translation is almost exactly line-for-line, with marginal numbers referring to the Oxford text. My version is not word-for-word, however, or syntax-for-syntax. I have often chosen to be faithful to the rhetorical emphasis of Euripides' word order at the expense of other sorts of accuracy.

Footnotes give information that will be helpful to readers with no classical background. Endnotes keyed to line numbers deal with major questions of interpretation or scholarship. Following the lead of previous editors, I have supplied a small number of stage directions.

The text I have translated rarely departs from Diggle's. I have everywhere used the classic commentary by Dodds and the new one by Seaford, with its novel and interesting interpretation.

I am grateful for advice to the publisher's anonymous reader and to my colleagues Barbara Goff and Paula Perlman. Thomas Palaima gave me valuable help with the introduction. Special thanks are due also to Philip Bobbitt, whose poetry group encouraged me to carry on translating verse into verse.

Introduction

The Play

Some time after Euripides' death around 407 B.C.E., his son produced three plays that were evidently his last work. One of these was *Bacchae,* a play unlike all others of his that have come down to us. No other literary work of the period goes so far in conveying the depth of feeling that belonged to the religious spirit of ancient Greece; none depicts a god behaving more savagely toward human beings. It is a play of many paradoxes, and it concerns a god whose eternal smile, fixed on the mask worn by the actor, can seem by turns to be warm, derisive, and menacing. It is a play about a kind of power that human beings must simply accept, that can lead them unwilling to sacrifice and initiation—or to terror and destruction. The play works by building, and at the same time resolving, conflicts between brute force and religion, between new and old, between savage and civilized, between city and mountain. Its choral poems veer from piercing beauty to cliché, its scenes move from comic to tragic, and its mood turns upside down, starting with hymns of devotion to a god of peace, but ending with a mother's lament over the body of a boy she has torn apart with her bare hands.

The place is Thebes, birthplace of the god Dionysus, a city of broad fields not far from imposing mountains, and the main action takes place where field and mountain meet, in the rough uplands and mountain pastures on the shoulders of Mt. Kithairôn. This action we never see, however, except through the eyes of the messengers who report to us the astounding things they have seen with their own eyes. The stage is set in the city, in front of the great house of the royal family, where a chorus of outlandishly dressed foreign women wheel and dance, singing cult songs of Dionysus. These Bacchae, as the women who celebrate Dionysus are called, are ushered on stage by the god himself.

Dionysus has many names in the play, and shows himself in many ways. He is Bacchus, Iacchus, and Evius—all names that evoke the joy of worshiping this god of peace and wine and dancing. He is also Bromius, the Thunderer, born in a blast of lightning, bringing terror against his enemies. He has come home to Thebes, where he was born of a human mother, and where his mother's sisters have long denied his divinity. He plans a horrible punishment for the royal family, a punishment that begins in the classic way—with the madness of the victims. Dionysus is most angry at his mother's sisters, his aunts, and these he drives into the mountains, where they dance themselves into frenzies, open springs of milk or wine in bare rock, and catch wild beasts, which they tear apart and eat raw—the legendary behavior of troops of women known as Maenads.

Meanwhile, back at the palace, there is a young king—very young for a king, no older than a college freshman—the son of one of Dionysus' own aunts, Agavê. The boy's name is Pentheus, and he thinks that because he is king he can put a stop to this new religion. Perhaps he, too, has been crazed by Dionysus, albeit in a very different way from his mother and aunts; or perhaps he has decided against Dionysus on rational grounds (as the chorus will imply). But, like many males of his time and place, he appears to be concerned mostly about maintaining order among women, for fear that they will give way to orgies of sex. Whatever the reason, Pentheus enacts a legendary resistance to Dionysus. Although the Greeks had worshiped Dionysus from the earliest times of which we have record (he is mentioned in Linear B texts), they celebrated him as a foreign god whose epiphanies annually startle and shake the traditional social order.

Pentheus first plans to take an army against the Maenads on the mountain, but Dionysus forestalls this action. The god takes the form of a beautiful young man from abroad with long blond curls and effeminate ways, who nevertheless has a powerful way with words. He talks Pentheus into going up the mountain in disguise, without an army, for purposes of observation before attempting military action. Perhaps this is sound tactics; perhaps it is an act of madness induced by the god; perhaps it simply expresses a set of desires latent in the young king's heart to see women at sexual play and even to be one of them. Perhaps it is all three. In any case, he allows Dionysus to dress him as a woman—a very revealing disguise, for it brings out the part of Pentheus' mind he is trying hardest to suppress—and lets the god lead him up the mountain to spy on the women. There they spy him, mistaking him for a wild beast, and tear him limb from limb, playing catch with pieces of him. His mother Agavê, in the lead, carries off his mangled head, and she brings it proudly into town under the delusion that it is the head of a lion she has slain with her own hands. She who failed to appreciate the divinity of her sister's son is now able to recognize the beastliness of her own boy—but not to see him as hers. Her punishment comes when she sees clearly, for the first time, what it is that she has been carrying, and realizes that she has killed her own son, brutally. Then she knows Dionysus for the potent god he is.

That is the pain Dionysus brings. But from the chorus we hear again and again of the delights he gave them—not merely wine and dance, but through initiation a joyful sense of freedom and clarity that would otherwise have been denied them. This is not news to the Athenians, who watched the play, like all plays, at a festival in celebration of Dionysus. They would have believed that Dionysus brought joy to Greece, and to Thebes first of all, when he came and initiated the Greeks in his religion. That is why they take delight in reenacting his coming to Greece and his overcoming resistance such as that of Pentheus.

#

That is the outline of the story. It is strange and horrible, yet it strikes a chord in many readers today, perhaps because of late twentieth-century anxiety about the resistance that is felt from science and technology against fantasy, emotion, and religion. The devout piety of the chorus suggests a parallel to Christianity; more parallels turn up under scrutiny, and these are not entirely accidental. Christian language and imagery were touched, even at a fairly early stage, by Dionysiac elements in Greek religion.[1]

---

1. Seaford (1996), p. 53, with notes, and Seaford (1997).

Some translations exploit the parallel through reminders of Christian liturgy in the choruses, but this is misleading in many ways. Christianity has an ethical message that is missing from Dionysus-worship, which seems to preach little but passivity and reverence toward the gods.

In a more secular vein, some productions of the play have used the imagery of pop music idols to bring Dionysus across to audiences of our time. We might visualize the encounter of the cousins Pentheus and Dionysus as a Mick Jagger in his prime running into a newly installed conservative dictator—but this would be helpful only if we could imagine a rock star who is able to call up a real earthquake, and a youthful dictator in command of an army willing to follow him against a religious cult.

However we try to visualize it, the *Bacchae* is more alien to modern experience than are most ancient plays. A proper understanding of the play must begin with that. To visualize the ancient staging of the play alone requires a stretch of imagination, and we shall need to know something of the cultural background of the *Bacchae* if we are to grasp the nature of the conflict between reason and religion to which the chorus frequently refers.

Cultural Background

Religion

The religious background of the play is elusive because it deals with rituals that were celebrated by women in secret, and because the worship of Dionysus was different in different cities and at different times. This play, for example, brings an Athenian sensibility to bear on what it represents as the foundation of a cult in Thebes; and although Thebes is neighbor to Athens, the two cities see themselves as opposed in culture. To make matters worse, ancient Greek literature tends to follow myth, rather than religious practice, leaving a disturbing gap between the two.

In the case of the *Bacchae* we must be careful to force neither our understanding of Greek religion to fit the play nor our understanding of the play to fit what we know of religion. Still, we have no text from the period that expresses religious feeling more movingly than the *Bacchae*, so we do have something to learn from the play about ancient Greece. And we have a great deal to learn about the play from a study of Dionysiac ritual, as Seaford (1994) has shown. Tragedy as a genre is informed by ritual practices, and the *Bacchae* especially so. Much of the plot of the play mirrors initiation ritual, although it is initiation gone wildly outside the norms of religion.

The gods of ancient Greek religion have distinct personalities in myth, but they also represent impersonal forces, and they serve as focus points for civic life as well, through the web of cult activities on which a city depends to maintain its social order. When the tragic plays were written, the Greek world consisted of independent city-states, such as Athens, each united internally and kept distinct from the others by shared laws and religious practices. True, individual worshipers may come under a god's protection, and individuals may even be allowed a temporary share in attributes of the god (as occurs in the rejuvenation of Cadmus and Tiresias). But it is primarily the city as a social unit that faces the gods in myth and in the theater that follows myth. Gods, for their part, make their appearances not to a few saints but in public, so as to assure a city of their power and to remind all human beings of mortality. The principal role of a god in myth and tragedy is to establish ascendancy.

Dionysus[2] is best known as a god of wine and intoxication, but he has also the power to give a blessed madness to his votaries by means other than drinking. In this play, his worshipers achieve ecstasy by dancing. Dionysus is a god of epiphany who is truly present to his worshipers in their frenzy, and whose work is mainly to make himself known to people. At the same time, paradoxically, he is a god of deception, as in theater, where masks are worn in his honor and gods impersonated; he is himself a god who has had enemies from birth and has always been able to hide from them. As a god of dynamic epiphanies, Dionysus becomes the eternal foreigner who is always making himself at home in the minds of the Greeks. Scholars used to think of him as a foreign god who became naturalized in Greece, but the truth is the opposite: he is a Greek god who came to be seen as foreign.

---

2. The religion of Dionysus is a difficult matter. For a primer, see Albert Henrich's article in the *Oxford Classical Dictionary* (1996, Hornblower and Spawforth, eds.), pp. 479–82, and relevant sections in Burkert's work (1985, 1987, and 1993). I have benefited also from Thomas Palaima (forthcoming). For an influential interpretation of Dionysus and his worship, see Detienne (1989).

The paradox of secrecy and epiphany belongs to Dionysus in virtue of his role in mystery religion—wearing masks for the uninitiated, but revealing himself totally to his votaries. Mystery religions were traditional in ancient Greece from at least the sixth century B.C.E. (Burkert 1987). They are defined by their use of initiation rites to reveal secret knowledge of the divine, and at the same time to mark a special relationship between an individual and a god. Initiates hope to lead more joyful inner lives than they did before, and they have better hopes for life after death than do the uninitiated (Plato, *Republic* 365a). Initiation is open to all, regardless of sex or age or citizenship, and so mystery religions provide a personal, egalitarian counterpoint to the public rituals of state religion. Democratic Athens was devoted to a mystery religion celebrated in nearby Eleusis—the Eleusinian mysteries of the goddess Demeter—and the Athenians protected these mysteries as belonging uniquely to their city. Acts of irreverence toward mysteries are especially offensive and punishable by law. Reverence itself, a cardinal virtue in the period, is most deeply the sense of holiness that comes over an individual during initiation.

As a god who presides over mysteries, Dionysus is both a life force on earth and a power in the underworld. Under the name Iacchus, Dionysus has a role in the Eleusinian mysteries by the side of Demeter (Henrichs 1990, p. 266), and in cities outside Athens he is celebrated in mysteries on his own or along with Orpheus. The religion of the chorus in the *Bacchae* is plainly a mystery religion based on initiation.[3] Dionysiac initiation and its trappings are seen in the play as preparations for the underworld (lines 857, 1157). The chorus of the *Bacchae* believes that initiation gives happiness in the present, along with a sense of freedom and a new clarity of understanding. To the uninitiated, the god may present a welter of competing images of himself, but initiates seem to have a simple and calm understanding of the god's power (line 40, with 21 and 75). Plato has Socrates speak of the therapeutic effect of initiation to Dionysus (*Phaedrus* 244e with 265b), and

---

3. That the religion of the play is to be seen as a mystery in the technical sense is vigorously but wrongly denied by Leinieks (1996, pp. 123–52). The evidence for the existence of Dionysus mysteries in this period is reviewed by Burkert (1993), and the case for mystery religion of the *Bacchae* is well made by Seaford (1996).

Sophocles hymns Dionysus as a god of healing in the *Antigone* (1115–52).

In some places outside Athens, Dionysus was celebrated secretly by groups of women dancing apart from men in the mountains, organized in bands (*thiasoi*) and led (so they believed) by Dionysus himself, who was always supposed to be present when worshiped. Athenian Maenads practiced their rites outside Attica. Inside Athens no fewer than seven public festivals were celebrated annually for Dionysus, two of which featured performances in the theater. All Athenian plays, in fact, were written to be performed as part of Dionysiac festivals (Pickard-Cambridge 1990).

In sum, the main powers of Dionysus are these: he is a god of wine, joy, and healing; he is a life force who protects the dead; and he is a master of disguise who knows how to make himself known by becoming truly present to those who follow him.

Madness and Control

Initiation rituals varied widely, but the one celebrated in the *Bacchae* seems to have been a journey through darkness to light, by way of a symbolic death or sacrifice, leading in the end to a full recognition of the god in his power. Votaries had to lose their wits through initiation in order to gain a properly reverent soundness of mind. That paradox of losing one's mind in order to gain it is fundamental to Dionysiac religion, even though celebrants evidently do not use words for madness (*mania*) of themselves. Plato's Socrates uses the language of initiation to glorify love in the *Phaedrus* as a form of madness that may lead to love of wisdom (244 ff., esp. 256a–b). The chorus in the *Bacchae* celebrates the joys of intoxication induced by wine or mountain dancing, and at the same time praises soundness of mind and all the calm and collected virtues that go with accepting the human condition. In almost one breath they praise self-control and letting go. But the sense of paradox in this cannot survive initiation. The wisdom of initiation is a serene acceptance that comes through letting go, an acceptance achieved through the frenzy of initiation. Such wisdom is totally incompatible with the wisdom of intellectuals such as Tiresias in this play, who have no intention of losing their wits—who try, indeed, to use their wits for exercising control over others.

Self-control was an important virtue to the Greeks. Plato's image for it is revealing: when a person has self-control it is as if he had a little man and some beasts inside his mind, with the man in firm command of the beasts (*Republic* 571c, 588b ff., *Phaedrus* 2453d ff.). To run wild, in Greek imagery, is to become like an animal—a terrifying possibility to the Greeks, except when it is part of a religious ritual that can lead to one's becoming more godlike.

Pentheus' fear of what women will do if they are allowed to run wild as Maenads without male supervision is only partly justified, and must therefore reveal something of his own suppressed desires. Maenadic rituals, though transgressing the usual norms, are historically orderly and benign—and so they are depicted in the *Bacchae* until they are interrupted by men. Then all hell breaks loose. The message of the play, as delivered by the chorus, is that peace, order, and control come through cult, and not through force of weapons (Pentheus' choice) or through the New Learning (which Tiresias represents). But the peace and order Dionysus offers Thebes has no place for the royal family that insulted him, and all we see of this new order in the *Bacchae* is the ground of Thebes polluted by a killing within the royal family.

Readers fascinated by what appears to be a cult of madness and ambiguity in the *Bacchae* should be reminded that in Athenian practice Dionysus-worship was part of an orderly civic life, which, in a paradoxical way, it supported. To Athenians, the wildness of Maenads and the danger that they represent are mainly the stuff of myth. But within the myth, the Maenads are truly a threat to Pentheus' control of Thebes, though not the sort of threat the young king imagines.

New Learning

"In the *Bacchae*," writes Geoffrey Kirk, "the shades of the great sophists Protagoras and Gorgias lurk behind scenes whose character may puzzle or disappoint the modern reader" (1979, p. 16). Of the new type of intellectual that became prominent in the latter half of the fifth century, the best known were the sophists, but there were also scientists, historians, and philosophers. The broad movement I am calling the New Learning became highly controversial in the fifth century and was the object of sharp satire in Aristophanes' *Clouds*. Aristophanes' targets included the new teaching of persuasive speech, along with a series of reasoned attacks on traditional religion, established law, and social custom. The chorus is alert to these intellectual trends and sees them as threats; it sees them, oddly, in Pentheus' untutored resistance to the god. Pentheus himself sees them, much less oddly, in the tactics of the young man whom Dionysus impersonates on stage. And the audience sees them in the clever but ineffective speech of Tiresias.

Much of the play is built on a contrast between two sorts of wisdom (Roux, 1970). On the one hand is the New Learning, which shows itself in fine speaking, is ambitious, and has little respect for tradition. On the other hand is the wisdom of acceptance, which leads to a quiet life, is modest, and resists innovation. The chorus speaks for the old wisdom and implicitly accuses Pentheus of being in the grip of the new; but Pentheus plans to defend old ways, attack Dionysus-worship as a dangerous innovation, and put down the clever sophist impersonated by Dionysus. Each side in the conflict identifies the other with the danger of the New Learning. The chorus treats Pentheus as guilty of New Learning by association, inasmuch as both he and science resist religion. Pentheus suspects Dionysus of sophistic tendencies because of his skill with words. And Dionysus is new and up-to-date, of course, new as today's New Learning, although he is also as old as traditions forgotten before Homer.

The Author

Euripides (c. 484–406 b.c.e.) came in the footsteps of Aeschylus and Sophocles and was mocked even in his maturity as a brash innovator and a threat to tradition.[4] When he was an old man over seventy he left Athens in anger or fear for the court of Macedon, where he died soon after. He became popular in the theater after his death and was admired by Aristotle as the most tragic of playwrights. We must be cautious in generalizing about his work because much is lost, and what remains is varied. He entered twenty-two sets of four plays each (winning only four first prizes); but of this enormous output, only nineteen plays survive, leaving no extant trilogy or tetralogy complete.

---

4. Aristophanes puts him on the side of the New Learning at *Clouds* 1353 ff.; see also his treatment of Euripides in *Frogs, Thesmophoriazousae,* and *Acharnians* (references in Seaford 1996, p. 18, n. 37).

Several themes of the *Bacchae* are prominent in the larger body of work. We will see that Euripides is well acquainted with the New Learning; he has picked up a good knowledge of rhetorical technique, and he is interested in many of the issues that were churning at the time, challenges to traditional ideas about gods and the place of women, the debate about constitutions, the relation of law to nature, and the value of rhetoric. But for all his intellectual interests, he gives full expression to the popular anti-intellectualism of the day. We cannot be sure where he stood on these issues, or even whether he took a stand on them, owing to his playwright's way of letting both sides speak and his tragedian's distrust of anyone who pursues a course single-mindedly.

Ancient and modern writers have made much of the criticism of gods that erupts in some of Euripides' plays. Typical is the protest we hear from Cadmus against Dionysus. "You are too severe," he says. "Anger does not become a god" (1346, 1348). But the gods of myth and literature are often angry, lashing out at each other or at human beings who do not deserve such treatment, and sometimes they do what is forbidden to mortals. Herakles, as a Euripidean character, refuses to believe such tales: "For a god, if he is a god, needs none of that; / but these stories the poets tell are dreadful" (*Herakles Mad* 1345–46). One Euripidean character has the effrontery to lecture Apollo on morality:

Since you are powerful, strive for virtue.
When anyone who is mortal
is by nature wicked, he is punished by the gods;
so how could it be just for you to write the laws
for us mortals, and then incur a charge of lawlessness
     yourselves?

                                                                    (Ion in *Ion* 439–43)[5]

Women's issues loom large in many of Euripides' plays, as he gives expression both to the fears men have of women's power

---

5. Translated by Gagarin and Woodruff (1995), as are all the texts quoted in this section. For Euripides' treatment of the gods, see also *Hecuba* 799 ff., for the idea that belief in gods is by *nomos*; testimony by Plutarch (*Amat.* 756b–c) on Fragment 480 from the *Melanippe*; fragments from *Bellerophon* 286 and 292.7; and the comment in *Thesmophoriazousae* 450 ff., in which Euripides is accused of teaching atheism.

and the anguish of women at their lack of freedom. Pentheus is sure he knows what evils women will turn to out of sight of men (215–32). In this he is like another of Euripides' young men who fear women, Hippolytus (*Hippolytus* 627–44). On the other side, Melanippe gives a beautiful defense of women against the reproaches of men in a lost play named after her:

> The reproaches men throw at women are groundless,
> their insults like the twang of an empty bowstring.
> Women are better than men, and I'll prove it.

She proceeds to do just that.[6] And an angry Euripidean Medea turns the tables on men, "I'd rather take my stand behind a shield [i.e., in battle] three times than bear one child," she says in the play named after her, concluding a lament on the lot of married women (230–51). Euripides must know that the women of the chorus in the *Bacchae* have reason to celebrate the freedom from men that they find in worshiping Dionysus, when they feel like a wild fawn escaping hunters (856–77); and he has the messenger observe this freedom when he likens the Maenads to draft animals that have left the decorated yoke of civilized marriage (1056).

As for politics, the chorus of the *Bacchae* is hostile to people who try to stand out from the crowd; generally, the cult of Dionysus is egalitarian and therefore especially appropriate for a democracy such as Athens. Euripides' contemporaries noticed the emphasis he gives to ordinary people in preference to well-born heroes in his writing. Claims to merit from high birth are emphatically rejected in a fragment of the *Alexander* (N 53), and we find outright hostility to tyranny in a number of plays. On the whole, Euripides seems supportive of both democracy and the law, as he shows in the constitutional debate he stages in the *Suppliant Maidens*. There, in defending the democratic laws of Athens to a herald from Thebes (a significant choice of origin for the monarchic side of the debate), Theseus says:

> Nothing means more evil to a city than a tyrant.
> First of all there will be no public laws
> but one man will have control by owning the law,

---

6. The entire speech is translated in Gagarin and Woodruff (1995, pp. 71–72), from D. L. Page *Select Papyri*, vol 3 (Loeb edition, 1941).

himself for himself, and this will not be fair.
When the laws are written down, then he who is weak
and he who is rich have equal justice . . .[7]

It is significant that Theseus supports democracy as a lawful form of government, and that the chorus of the *Bacchae* speaks up for common people and the law at the same time. The chorus opposes Pentheus both because he is a monarch and because it thinks he is acting as if he were above the law. In writing as if lawful democracy is a real possibility, Euripides is squaring off against those enemies of democracy who slander it as a lawless tyranny by the lower classes over everyone else. Critics of democracy in this period tend to identify it with lawlessness (*anomia*) and use the word "good-law-government" (*eunomia*) as code for oligarchy, which means government by a few rich and well-born leaders. Because Euripides contrives to include thoughtful support for democratic institutions in the *Suppliant Maidens,* even though it is not required by the plot, I conclude that the sentiment comes from Euripides himself.

He seems to take a stand on the controversy about law and nature as well. In the late fifth century, reformers begin to appeal to nature against law—to the idea that nature has established permanent universal norms, whereas the laws made by human beings serve only relative to the interests of those who make them.[8] Their case seems stronger in the Greek language, which at this period does not yet distinguish between written law and social custom; one word, *nomos,* serves for both. Dionysus hints at this relativism when he defends the good sense of foreigners by saying, "They just have different customs (*nomoi*)" (484). But the evidence seems to show that Euripides gives little play to the idea that nature and law might come into conflict. The chorus of the *Bacchae* insists on obedience to laws that are both long established and natural (895–96, on which see my endnote), and Jocasta in the

---

7. *Suppliant Maidens* 429–34 in the debate of 399–456. See also fragments 172N and 608N (Gagarin and Woodruff, pp. 70 and 72).
8. Thrasymachus, in Plato's *Republic,* is the most accessible representative of such a view (338*c* ff.), along with Callicles in the *Gorgias* (483*b*). Although both works are fiction, such ideas are probably held by a number of intellectuals at the end of the fifth century.

Phoenician Women declares, "Fairness is by nature the law (or norm) for human beings" (538). Democrat he may be, but Euripides appears to be sympathetic to those who defend tradition against change.

The anti-intellectualism of the *Bacchae* is a corollary of conservative populism, an attack on those who try to stand out by means of intelligence or cultivation, and a defense against innovation. Perhaps Euripides is responding in these passages to criticism that had been leveled against him for being too clever to suit popular taste. But he is also expressing an anxiety that was common in Greek culture at that time, about the dangers of raising oneself too high by intellectual means. The *Suppliant Maidens* expresses this in a passage that is strikingly similar to the famous "Ode to Man" from Sophocles' *Antigone* (365 ff.): "Our minds keep striving to be stronger than the god" (216–18). There is a burlesque of clever people's attitudes toward the gods in Euripides' only surviving satyr-play; and this too plays to popular dislike of intellectuals.[9] Not surprisingly, it is women who suffer the most for showing signs of intelligence, and Euripides does not hesitate to bring this injustice into the open.[10]

Euripides' general sympathies in the great debates of his time are now fairly clear, but I have left open the question of Euripides' attitude toward religion and the criticism of it by some teachers of the New Learning. This is the main ideological issue raised by the *Bacchae*, and I will return to it when I review general interpretations of the play.

Ancient Tragic Theater

Ancient Greek tragedies were performed in a dense clump of plays before an enormous audience at Athenian festivals in honor of Dionysus. The principal ancestors of tragedy were religious ritual (about which we know all too little) and narrative poetry (of

---

9. "Wealth is god to the wise," says Cyclops to Odysseus, defending his practice of eating human flesh. "Whether it wants to or not, the earth by necessity gives birth to the sort of thing that fattens my animals. I sacrifice to no one but myself and the greatest of divinities, this belly of mine, but never to a god" (*Cyclops* 316, 332–34).
10. *Medea* 294–302. "I hate a clever woman," says Hippolytus (640).

which we have excellent examples). This ancestry explains two features of the plays that seem odd to modern audiences—the chorus and the messengers.

Chorus

Dancing and singing on the part of the chorus are at the center of an ancient tragedy, and although the role of the chorus wanes slightly during the fifth century, it is restored to great importance in the *Bacchae*. The chorus sings in lyric meters that cannot be reproduced by English verse, because ancient rhythmic patterns depend on length of syllable, rather than on emphasis. Sung lyrics are accompanied by the music of an *aulos* (conventionally translated "flute") a reed instrument ancient audiences found especially arousing emotionally. The meters alone evoke feeling, and this was reinforced in the *Bacchae* by drums, probably carried by the chorus itself.

Messengers

Only the verbal drama is enacted on stage, and the audience sees directly only debates, arguments, speeches, and conversations. Physical action takes place offstage and is reported to the audience. In the *Bacchae* this device is especially prominent; even such easily stageable events as Dionysus' arrest and Pentheus' cross-dressing are performed offstage. Some actions are related by characters, with a slant in each case that is appropriate to the teller (215–20, 616–37, 433–42); other events are brought to life by messengers (677–768 and 1043–1148). Each of the two messengers in the *Bacchae* has a gripping story to tell, and tells it out of character—elegantly and with near omniscience. At times their speeches remind us of their ancestry in epic narrative, as in the perfectly timed metaphor for the miracle of the fir tree (1066–68). The verse form uses quick-flowing iambics, however, rather than the slower dactyls of epic poetry.

Staging

Actors and chorus are all male, wearing masks to indicate the parts they play. There are only three actors to a play at the time of the *Bacchae,* up from one in the earliest tragedies. This limitation gives the happy result, for example, that the same performer would enact the preparations for Dionysiac sacrifice or initiation (in the role of Pentheus) and afterward the return and enlightenment (in the role of Agavê).

The performance is held outdoors in a circular space (the "orchestra") around a symbolic hearth for the dancing, and behind that on a platform with the facade of a building. In a play as late as the *Bacchae* the scenery might be painted to represent the house of the Theban royal family. Part of the house is shaken down during lines 576–603 (the "palace miracles"); scholarly opinion is divided over whether such miracles would be shown onstage. The audience certainly hears thunder, lightning, and earthquake described, and sees the abject reaction of the chorus. But the audience itself does not need to see or hear the miracles. They are the way the god announces his divinity and could be taken (like other signs and portents) on faith by an ancient audience (see the endnote on lines 576–603).

Time and Place

The setting for many tragic plays is Thebes,[11] and the time is before recorded history, soon after the founding of the city by Cadmus. Thebes is close enough to Athens to be interesting, but far enough away culturally and in other ways to allow a playwright to air horrifying subjects safely in that setting. There were also patriotic reasons for setting disaster stories in Thebes. Thebes is Athens' inland neighbor, but the Thebans sided against Athens twice—with Persia in the Persian Wars, and with Sparta in the war that was winding down to Athens' defeat at the very time Euripides was writing the play. Athens, moreover, was a democracy, and Dionysus was the most democratic of ancient Greek divinities.[12] Thebes was never friendly to democracy, and it may have given the Athenians special pleasure to enact the violent arrival of their democratic god at the doorstep of a monarch.

---

11. On the meaning of Thebes in Athenian tragedy, see Zeitlin (1990, especially p. 145) and Zeitlin (1993).
12. Lines 421–23 with Dodds (1960, pp. 127–28).

Plot

The action of the *Bacchae* is generated throughout by decisions the characters have made, usually under the influence of persuasion. Although the play contains a passing reference to the assent of Zeus "long ago" (1349), fate and divine decree operate in the background, if at all. Fate may drive the stories that lie behind many well-known Greek tragedies, but the actual plays generally stage scenes in which one character tries to persuade another what to do or to believe, and the audience must believe that the characters have real choices to make. The *Bacchae* fits this familiar pattern, turning as it does on Dionysus' persuading Pentheus to dress as a woman and to spy on the Theban women in the mountain (lines 787–846). Dionysus plays simultaneously on Pentheus' explicit commitment to doing the right thing as a soldier and his suppressed desire to explore the more vulnerable feminine side of his personality. To this end Dionysus exploits the ambiguity of the Greek word *stolê,* which means "outfit" in either the sense of military equipment or of a woman's dress. In other ways, too, Dionysus is a perfect sophist, and we see Pentheus succumb not to his fate, but to Dionysus' mastery of the art of words.

The Characters of the *Bacchae*

The principal characters are all members of the royal house of Cadmus; the minor characters, from ordinary walks of life, are generally more sympathetic. (For the royal family tree, see p. xlv; for Euripides' democratic views, see p. xix.)

Dionysus as a Character

On stage he probably wore the same mask in every scene, a young god with a smiling or laughing face. But different characters see him differently, and some readers have thought that his essence is ambiguity. Early portrayals of the god show him as a mature man, strong and bearded, but by the time of the *Bacchae* the trend has set in for painters and sculptors to give him a soft and youthful appearance.

First, we meet the god himself—well, not quite himself: he is in disguise as a human being, a priest or celebrant of the Bacchic religion, but he tells us he is a god, and we hear that he is an angry one. Second, we hear of him from the chorus, to whom he is a source of delight, release, and freedom, at the same time as he is a fearsome power to whom they pray for justice in their distress. Third, we see him as Pentheus does, as an effeminate foreigner with a gift for clever speaking. The chorus see what Pentheus sees—a beautiful young man in Bacchic costume. They do not recognize him as the god, but take him as their "comrade in the sacred dance" (547), and later as "our great light in dancing to Bacchus" (608), and as a protector to the foreign women (612).[13] Pentheus, when he emerges in women's dress, sees Dionysus more accurately, as a bull (920). Dionysus will make a fourth appearance in the end, revealing himself to the Thebans as a god, and in this role Cadmus will see him as ruthless and petulant, not caring if the punishment he exacts is excessive. On one occasion we hear the god's own voice, shouting offstage, at the beginning of Scene Three (575–604), and we hear of such a shout from the messenger (1079–81).

When Dionysus speaks in disguise as a young man he works through double meanings or ambiguities. These allow him to fulfill Pentheus' expectations of a clever speaker while maintaining the calm authority of a god. When he speaks as a god he is clear and direct, pedantic, unfeeling, and strong. During most of the play, however, the audience sees him the way Pentheus does, as a human being who "acts and talks like a sophist" (Henrichs, 1986, p. 395).

The real Dionysus, we must suppose, is the one whom the chorus members know in their hearts as a source of joy; his many appearances, whether ambiguous or terrifying, seem to matter only to those who do not know him (line 478).

Chorus

The chorus of women from Asia probably numbers fifteen, and the actors who play them are citizens of Athens. On one theory, they are young men about to begin military training—just the age of King Pentheus. They play the parts of mature women, however, who are foreign to Thebes and to Greece. The kind word for this status is *xenai* (guests, strangers), but they are also called *barbaroi*

---

13. In this role he does not correspond to anyone known to have taken part in Dionysus-worship. The women danced alone (Henrichs, 1984).

(foreigners). Their outlandishness would be visible in their costumes, though the basics of their Bacchic paraphernalia would be familiar to Athenians.

They dance with precision and sing poems of unearthly beauty to the accompaniment of flute and drum. What Euripides wrote for this chorus is extraordinary for its power, its length, and its use of original imagery. It includes some of the most beautiful poetry written in ancient Greek.

The members of this chorus are not agents in the tragic action. They observe and comment, and their comments are wise with the common sense of good Athenian citizens. This is odd from a dramatic point of view, and even more surprising than the convention that allows them to speak Greek. For this chorus represents a foreign intrusion onto Greek soil—but an intrusion that stands for traditional Greek values. Poetry had actually been treating foreigners as consummate Greeks since Homer's depiction of the Trojans, and this is one of the most attractive and unusual features of Greek culture. Although ancient Greeks had a strong sense of themselves as separate from, and superior to, foreigners, their literature took them across boundaries with a sympathy that expressed itself in endowing foreigners with Greek language and customs. The paradox of the chorus mirrors the paradox of Dionysus himself, who is both a foreigner, as we saw, and a returning native.

Euripides' chorus celebrate the passive wisdom of initiates and the virtues of ordinary folk. They castigate those who wish to stand out (e.g., at line 429) or who attempt to use their wisdom actively for control (395–96). In their religion they resist every kind of superiority on the part of an elite (897–912). Their attitude may reflect the democratic sympathies of Euripides and his Athenian audience, but there may be ritual reasons as well that demand the destruction of a royal family for the survival of the city (Seaford, 1994, esp. p. 344).

Would Euripides, then, have expected his audience to side entirely with the chorus? Some scholars, especially Dodds, have remarked on the difference between the chorus on stage and the Maenads on the mountain—the sober foreigners in the heart of the city and the crazed natives in the wild woods. The chorus are the more domestic Bacchants, yet they are the true initiates, unlike the new converts from Thebes. The Theban women are not allowed to see clearly, and their ecstasy is itself not a reward (as it is for the chorus) but a punishment.

We must not be seduced by the chorus, however. Their religion is not all sweetness and light. "The lust for blood . . . their pitiless, avid response to tragic events—these do not permit us to believe we have found in them a safe and civilized Dionysianism."[14] Maenadic rituals did not occur in Athens, perhaps because it was not permitted; and even Plato, who sets a high value on divinely inspired enthusiasm, is suspicious of the ecstasy of Maenads (*Republic* 365a and *Laws* 815c–d). An ancient audience would not have assumed that Thebes was better off for the introduction of Maenadism.[15]

Tiresias

Tiresias, the seer, is legendary for his ability to tell the future through divination, and has been treated with respect by Sophocles. Divination, however, fell into disrespect after the Athenians lost the greater part of their military strength in Sicily by following the advice of diviners in 413 b . c . e . Surprisingly, Euripides makes little of this in the *Bacchae*, except to have Tiresias deny that his prognostication is based on his art.

As a diviner, he represents Apollo, who has authority for the founding of religions.[16] Yet Tiresias does not seem to speak for that authority here and does not play the part of diviner at all. The cleverness with which he speaks is undisguised by his disclaimers; it is not the "subtle ecclesiastical wisdom" claimed by one scholar[17]; rather, it is the art of the New Learning, incongruously put to the service of defending what its adherents were best known for attacking—religion. His speech teems with word-plays and other reminders of the sophisticated rhetoric taught by sophists.

---

14. Nussbaum, speaking for many modern readers, in Williams (1990, p. xiv). See also Kirk (1970, p. 9) criticizing the "white Maenadism" of Dodds.

15. Halloran (1996, p. 729), criticizing Seaford.

16. Plato will appeal to the oracle of Apollo to determine the religious practices of his ideal city (*Republic* 427b, *Laws* 738b).

17. Winnington-Ingram (1947, p. 41).

Cadmus

Himself an immigrant to Thebes, Cadmus has married his daughter Agavê to a man who was born from the earth, a true native, Echion. He himself comes from Sidon, very foreign, very far away, and this play celebrates the value of foreign intrusions by treating the earthborn as the real threat to Thebes and its traditions. Cadmus claims that the dance rejuvenates him (as Dionysiac ritual is supposed to do) and indeed he is younger after his journey to the mountain and back. He begins as a garrulous, almost senile, old man, very conventional, and ends as a strong tragic figure, able to recover his grandson's body, help Agavê recover her sanity, and complain frankly to the god over the excessive punishment his family has been made to suffer.

Pentheus

A boy between sixteen and twenty years old,[18] Pentheus is at a transitional age, when most boys are negotiating the change from a passive to an active role in society, about the time of military training. We cannot be sure what he was like before his cousin Dionysus came to town; perhaps he has already been crazed by Dionysus into a state in which he can see no further than resistance to the new cult.

He is trying very hard to be a good soldier, and Dionysus cleverly exploits this by giving him a military excuse to dress up as a woman, thus perhaps bringing unconscious desires past the boy's internal censor. Under the influence of Dionysus—as the effect either of rhetoric or of magic—Pentheus regresses to passivity and to childhood, longing for the softness of his mother's arms.

In the end he will do what a good soldier does: give up his life for his people. His death will satisfy the anger of Dionysus against Thebes, and his sacrifice will be marked by some of the features of

---

18. For Pentheus' youthfulness, see lines 274, 974, 1185–87, and 1254. Most scholars agree, as do the images of Pentheus in ancient vase paintings. Leinieks alone holds that Pentheus must be represented as a man of mature years, so as to be felt as a real threat (1996, p. 199 ff.). But an adolescent in command of an army is dangerous enough. On interpretations of Pentheus as a character, see Oranje (1984). Zeitlin (1996) offers insights about his feminization.

the killing of a scapegoat, although dying at the hands of his mother brings a dreadful pollution to the royal family, which now must go into exile. His name means "grief," and he has certainly brought grief to his family. What has he brought to his city? Perhaps Thebes remains polluted at the play's end; perhaps it has been redeemed by the young king's sacrifice, and blessed by the foundation of a joyful new religion.[19]

Messengers

The play's messengers are not really characters at all, but narrators endowed with the reliability of omniscience. The first messenger has a reason to tell his tale to Pentheus, but the second one has no motive whatever to speak to the women from Asia, and his speech lies outside the action of the play.

Agavê

Agavê did not believe her sister's story, and now she is terribly punished. She is more stage prop than dramatic character, this mad woman who arrives waving her son's severed head in her arms and soon after submits to therapy from her father. She does not act, she is acted upon, and yet she must be accepted by the audience as a real person who is to be pitied more than any other in the play, despite the absurdity of her situation. Without a mask, the part would be very difficult to bring off in serious theater.

Interpretations of the *Bacchae*

The play is disturbing on many levels. Most interpreters have sought the comfort of a message from the playwright, but they have not agreed on what this would be. The *Bacchae* wears as many faces to its scholars as Dionysus seems to do within its action. On stage, different characters see Dionysus differently; the same has been true for scholars in libraries and studies. And although the characters on stage might reach consensus about the

---

19. Seaford argues well for the optimistic conclusion (1994, 1996), but he has not convinced all scholars (Halloran, 1996, Esposito, 1998, p. 14, and Segal, 1997, pp. 356–58).

god once they are initiated into his mystery, we moderns have no such hope. As long as the play survives and there are scholars to discuss it, they will disagree among themselves. They are on more secure ground when they notice each other's deficiencies than when they launch into their own interpretations. But all seem to agree on the greatness of the play.

I begin with a survey of trends in interpretation, at the cost of much oversimplification. Many views combine several of the trends I discuss, and all are more sophisticated than I can indicate in these short summaries.

1. *Recantation: Euripides turns in favor of religion*

From ancient times, many students of Euripides have believed that he attacked religion in his earlier plays (p. xviii), was severely criticized for these attacks,[20] and came to repent in old age, when he wrote the *Bacchae*. The play, on this view, serves as Euripides' recantation ("palinode") to the gods and his defense to the people of Athens on an unofficial charge of irreverence. The interpretation prevailed until late in the nineteenth century. In this century, however, scholars have almost unanimously rejected the idea that Euripides had such a change of heart. Close study of earlier plays shows that he had always recognized the power of the irrational and the failure of rationalism to defeat it.[21] Modern critics have also pointed out, rightly, that there is nothing in the *Bacchae* to counter the moral criticism of mythological religion that found expression in Euripides' earlier plays. The triumph of Dionysus here is no less morally disturbing than is the victory of Aphrodite in the *Hippolytus* (Dodds, 1960, p. xlii, xlv).

On the other hand, the *Bacchae* contains a uniquely sustained attack against the rationalism of the New Learning, and it expresses the alternative to such rationalism more clearly than any other ancient work. This much life, therefore, remains in the old interpretation: the *Bacchae* is uniquely religious among Euripides'

---

20. E.g., at Aristophanes *Thesmophoriazousae,* line 450 ff., Aristophanes puts Euripides on the side of the New Learning at *Clouds* 1353 ff.; see also his treatment in *Frogs* and *Acharnians* (references in Seaford 1996, p. 18 n. 37).

21. E.g., Nussbaum (1990, p. xxii). The failure of Hecuba's well-crafted rationalist argument in the *Trojan Women* (at lines 969 ff.) is a case in point.

plays through its use of the chorus to express, at uncommon length, their reverence for the god.

Nietzsche, on weak grounds, accepts a version of the recantation interpretation.[22] His well-known theory about the creative tension between Apollo and Dionysus is largely based on his reading of this play. He has, of course, set us his own problem in interpretation, and scholars have debated which side Nietzsche is on, the Apollinian or the Dionysiac. But Nietzsche believes that tragic art arises only when each of the two gods comes somehow to speak the language of the other; the Apollinian need for control and individuation in ancient Greek culture merely shows how powerful is the undercurrent of the irrational, and the two gods are in balance at the moment of tragic culture in Greece. Nietzsche was a brilliant, though imaginative, classical scholar, with an extraordinary blend of knowledge and insight, but he was also a philosopher, and his interest in the two gods comes not only from his scholarship, but from themes with which he is wrestling in Schleiermacher.

2. *Morality: Euripides inveighs against myth on moral grounds*

Scholars in the later nineteenth century began to see the play as a moral condemnation of the image of Dionysus as presented in myth.[23] The best, and most moderate, descendant of such interpretations is that of Winnington-Ingram, which is still widely read and worthy of respect. "Euripides," he says, "makes the beauty of Dionysus skin-deep, turns his wisdom into cleverness and his calm control into the calculating pursuit of a personal vendetta" (p. 27). Winnington-Ingram sustains this view without overlooking the complexity of the play; he admits that Dionysus is made to appear both beautiful and dangerous but stresses the order of these appearances: Dionysus-worship may be seductive as seen through the eyes of the chorus in the beginning, but by the end of the play this impression should be more than balanced by a sense of the horrible dangers that attend on its extravagant joys (p. 11).

---

22. *Birth of Tragedy* (1870). On the recantation interpretation in general see Dodds (1960, p. xl); on Nietzsche's use of it, see Henrichs's highly critical essay (1986) and Segal's partial defense (1997, pp. 359–62).

23. Winnington-Ingram (1947, repr. 1969); see also references in Dodds (1960, p. xli).

Most recent critics have rejected this view also. If the play were a moral condemnation of Dionysus, then we would expect it to make a martyr of Pentheus, but this it does not do.[24] Most recently, Seaford has argued that it would be impossible for the play to be seen as critical of Dionysus in a festival celebrating that very god: "The play is not in any way an attack, as some have supposed, on Dionysiac cult. That the citizens of Athens continue to perform collective cult . . . is essential for the cohesion of the polis" (1996, p. 50). He believes, however, that the play may have helped Athenians resolve their tensions about the arrival of new foreign cults (p. 52). Seaford's case is not entirely convincing. Athenian theater was not required always to treat its patron god with reverence, for audiences accepted slapstick comedy at Dionysus' expense in Aristophanes' *Frogs* (also performed at a religious festival). In any case, we cannot be sure that it was Euripides' dying wish to have the *Bacchae* reverently received in performance at Athens.

Any fully adequate interpretation, however, must deal in some way with the moral problem posed by Dionysus' excessive anger against his human family, and it should explain why Euripides puts emphasis on this excess.

3. *Rationalism: Euripides refutes miracle-religion*

Some scholars early in this century developed an ingenious reading of the play as showing up the absurdity of belief in miracles. On this view, audiences should see that the part of Dionysus is played by a votary who is merely impersonating the god, and that the miracles are merely staged to support the cult. This interpretation of the play has been much discussed, but it will not bear up under study of a text that does nothing explicit to cast suspicion on the god's reality. In any event the interpretation makes nonsense of the staging, as the text allows no way to show that the miracles (which must be represented in some fashion in the play) are being staged as—well, as merely being staged. "The final condemnation of these bleak ingenuities," writes Dodds (1960, p. l), "is, for me at least, that they transform one of the greatest of all tragedies into a species of donnish witticism (a witticism so ill-

---

24. Kirk (1979, p. 8) and Dodds (1960, p. xliii).

contrived that it was twenty-three centuries before anyone saw the point)."[25]

4. *Irrationalism: the play warns, on psychological grounds, against the danger of trying to suppress the irrational*

Some readers have found a contemporary meaning in the play. Dodds speaks of "the dangerous Bacchism which descends as a punishment on the too respectable and sweeps them away against their will" (1951, p. 272). "The moral of the *Bacchae*," he says elsewhere, "is that we ignore at our peril the demand of the human spirit for Dionysiac experience. . . . In himself, Dionysus is beyond good and evil; for us, as Tiresias says (314–18), he is what we make of him" (1960, p. xlv). This is a very attractive line; undergraduates take to it very naturally, and there is certainly some truth to it. Poetic justice is satisfied when Pentheus, with his fear and loathing of the opposite sex, dresses voluntarily as a woman and emulates their femininity. And we can understand the event rationally, leaving the divine out of the story, if we suppose that there is a psychological force that rises from inside Pentheus to lead him to destruction.

Observations of psychological truth *in* the play, however, should not be mistaken for interpretations *of* the play. Certainly, the play warns against trying to suppress the irrational; but the grounds it repeatedly cites for this warning are religious, not psychological, and the goal the chorus praises for human life is not mental health as such, but the well-being that flows from reverence.

A second count against the psychological interpretation is that it is no kindness to Euripides to attribute to him a theory that is false. Young men with Pentheus' prurient mixture of fear and curiosity about women are common in all ages, but few of them end as badly as Pentheus. As for the respectable women of Thebes, we have had considerable experience with respectability in modern times, and we have not found that it is liable to break out in anything like Maenadism, although perhaps we should be delighted if it did. Kirk's objection to Dodds is on target: "The

---

25. The authors of this view are Norwood and, most famously, Verrall. For references and discussion, see Dodds (1960, pp. xlviii–l).

usual punishment of those who resist emotion, literature notwith-
standing, is not hysteria in the raw, a violent but temporary attack
of the emotion that is being suppressed, but rather a kind of psy-
chosis whose operation takes on a very different outward form
from that of the suppressed emotion" (1970, p. 12).

In other areas, the *Bacchae* comes closer to common human
experience. Several scholars have observed that there is psycho-
analytical truth in the crucial scenes of the play in which Pentheus
and Agavê are changed by their handlers, Dionysus and Cadmus
respectively.[26] Perhaps Euripides was consciously wise about
such matters, or perhaps he was carried by the wisdom inherent
in initiatory ritual, which both scenes mimic.

5. *Tragic truth: the play honestly represents unresolved tensions in*
   human life

On this view, there is no single message to the play at all. The
Bacchae shows the beauty and danger of Dionysus-worship inex-
tricably linked in tragic conflict. Dionysus expresses tension simply by being the sort of god he is, a compound of opposites and a
crasher of boundaries. Whether such tension is cause for grief or
celebration is one of those questions that this interpretation must
leave unanswered: the tensions are here, in our lives; the play
shows this and says no more.

> In his best plays Euripides used these conflicts not to make
> propaganda but as a dramatist should, to make tragedy out of
> their tension. . . . His favorite method is to take a one-sided
> point of view, a noble half-truth, to exhibit its nobility, and
> then to exhibit the disaster to which it leads its blind ad-
> herents—because it is, after all, only part of the truth. (Dodds,
> 1960, p. xlvi, citing Virginia Woolf on the *Antigone*)

This is plainly right, and should be part of any reading of the play.

> Euripides was conscious of the ambivalence of Dionysus, of
> the contrast between the god of pleasant ecstasy on the one

---

26. Seaford (1996, pp. 33–34). See in particular Devereux (1970), Sale
(1972), and Parsons (1988).

hand, and the god of destructive powers on the other, and of the moral and social instability of those who excessively devoted themselves to him. (Kirk 1979, p. 10)

If so, there is no answer to the traditional question of whether the poet is for or against Dionysus (Segal 1982; expanded edition 1997, p. 20). Even at the end we are left with contrary valences: the play gives us only the illusion of an epiphany, writes Segal. "This god theatrically stages his own triumph. His victorious procession leaves behind as much chaos as coherence" (Segal, p. 346). Segal's grand full-scale discussion of the play along these lines is intricate and difficult to summarize. Serious students of the *Bacchae* will devour it entire and not tear it to pieces. It was written at a time when the finding of ambiguities was fashionable in literary criticism. Now, sixteen years later, many readers will agree with Seaford's caution that the ambiguity of the play is controlled and the tension resolved at least in terms of the city's commitment to Bacchic ritual (1994, pp. 393–95); but Segal's development of the idea of metatragedy has made a lasting impression on scholars: several scenes in the *Bacchae* reflect on the nature of theater itself, and on tragedy in particular (Chapter 7).

More recently, and along slightly different lines, Nussbaum reveals how the play brings home to the audience the inescapable risks involved in judgment or allegiance. Her view is so delicately nuanced and, I think, so important, that I will quote from her at some length:

[The play is remarkable for] . . . the depiction of boundaries that might have seemed especially firm and reliable as fluid, mobile, suddenly shifting. What had seemed foul turns out to be beautiful. . . . Norms, constraints, shift as easily and silently as the snakes these women wear, sinuous and sudden. Nothing stands still for assessment. (Nussbaum 1990, p. xvi)

The chorus so strangely links ecstasy and transcendence with the praise of moderation and keeping one's place . . . because to know that we are followers of and constituted by that ecstasy is to know as well that we cannot firmly claim a dignity that we might have wished to claim for ourselves: the dignity of reason, of firm morality. We keep our place—not simply as different from the divine, but also as its subjects, subject to its beauty and its danger. (Nussbaum 1990, p. xxxvii)

Unlike other adherents of the ambivalence interpretation, Nussbaum believes that the play carries at least the suggestion of a message, that "any reasonably rich and complex life, sexual or social, is lived in a complex tension between control and yielding, risking always the loss of order" (Nussbaum, 1990, p. xxxix).

Rich as it is, her account passes over the role of Bacchic rituals in maintaining the sane and orderly life of the city. This, I suppose, is because she does not recognize the power of initiation and ritual over tension and paradox. The chorus of initiates links two feelings that strike noninitiates as contrary—ecstasy and moderation—but these are in fact united in the experience of the initiate, and they are united without a residue of tension. The chorus is at peace with itself.

Peace comes easily to the chorus because they are not represented as tied to the complexity of a Greek city. They are foreigners, reveling in the simplicity of a religion that has set them free to travel with no duties of citizenship. Such a life is unimaginable to a Greek of the fifth century. There can be no such thing as a permanent holiday in real civic life; but there are holidays nonetheless in Athens, and the play does seem to promise a release from tension for those who worship Dionysus—at least at the time they celebrate his mysteries.

6. *Ritual. Tragedies enact ritual sacrifice and initiation in a perverse form*

This thesis is developed with subtlety and in detail by Seaford throughout his commentary; the general theory is laid out in *Reciprocity and Ritual* (1994). In civic life, if Seaford is right, celebration of Dionysus is essential to the unity of the Greek city, so that the destruction of Pentheus is "a social necessity," and the grisly end of the play would justify neither religious pessimism nor an attack on religion.[27] If Seaford's general line is right, then no an-

---

27. Seaford (1996, pp. 50 and 255). Halloran (1996) and Esposito (1998, p. 14) do not believe that the thesis is emotionally plausible. Leinieks

cient audience would have made much of the tensions that delight recent scholars; such tensions are matters only of appearance, due to a modern failure to see how initiation eases tension at its source. Initiation replaces the conflicting appearances of the god with a single, consistent, and captivating experience.

Seaford's work, though controversial, is of great importance on points that cannot be summarized, because it works (more than other interpretations) by accounting for specific elements in the text. I have brought some of this out in the endnotes, but serious readers will have to consult Seaford's commentary themselves. They need not know Greek to do so with understanding. The reward is an inoculation against reading modern moral and religious concerns too readily into this text, and a new delight in appreciating its remoteness from our own culture.

7. Political interpretations

Leinieks emphasizes the link between Dionysus and political liberation, along with ideas of universality and unity among human beings that anticipate those of the Stoics (1996, p. 327 ff.). Esposito believes that the play exposes the "brutal realities of power politics in the late fifth century." "Dionysus and Pentheus seem to embody the anger of jealous city-states," he observes, reading into fifth-century attitudes the harsh judgments of Thucydides (1998, p. 18).

A modern reader who knows Greek history can hardly help making such connections, but they are not helpful in answering specific questions about the text. Why, for example, is Tiresias suddenly in the *Bacchae* represented not as a diviner but as an intellectual? No playwright, not even Euripides, has done this before. Why does the chorus castigate Pentheus for the faults of intellectuals, when the faults he has shown are quite the opposite? Why does Dionysus speak like a sophist when he confronts Pentheus? None of the interpretations I have reviewed so far offers any help with these questions, which suggest that the *Bacchae* has something to do with the conflict between religion and the new intellectuals, a conflict that raged in Athens at the time this play was written, leading, apparently, to the execution of Socrates. Such connections were noticed by Roux (1970, p. pp. 49–55) and

---

(wrongly, I think) attacks Seaford's view that Dionysus-worship in the *Bacchae* is represented as a mystery religion (1996, pp. 153–75).

Arrowsmith (1959, p. 145). They are far more important to the text than the political observations of Leinieks and Esposito, and they will be the basis for my own account of the play.

Interpreting the *Bacchae:* Translator's Conclusion

Most interpreters ask after Euripides' aim in writing the play, but this is a peculiar question. Could we give a useful, coherent account of Shakespeare's aim in writing *Troilus and Cressida?* I doubt it. We cannot be sure that Euripides had any other aim in writing the *Bacchae* than to write this play—the one we have in front of us, more or less—and I think I have already interpreted it in one way by translating it as I have. We would have to interpret it in yet another way if, as a group of actors, we were to put it on stage and choose how to bring it to life. This second level of interpretation I have not attempted, although I have raised some questions in the endnotes and introduction that actors would want to answer: Is Tiresias' speech a comical parody of high-blown rhetoric? Is Pentheus sane when he begins to be drawn to the idea of an observation patrol to the mountain? Is he bewitched or is he persuaded? When Dionysus takes human form in the opening scenes, does he have the dignity of a god? How far does Cadmus break away from his senility in the last scene of the play? All these and more require answers, but they do not bear directly on the question of the playwright's aim in writing the play.

Other questions are more promising. In one version of the story of Dionysus' arrival in Thebes, Pentheus does take an army up the mountain and is defeated in battle by Maenads. Was it Euripides' idea to change the received myth, or was his version already a commonplace in Athens—to forget the battle of Theban troops and Maenads on the mountainside, and instead to have the contest fought and won in the mind of the young king? If the new plot were Euripides' invention, that would tell us that the writer's aim was, among other things, psychological by choice; but it is fairly clear that Euripides did not make up his version of the story.[28]

---

28. "It has emerged beyond doubt that the myth of Pentheus dramatized in the *Bacchae* does not derive from a single individual. Its uniqueness is rather as the only detailed account we possess of a kind of sacrifice that can be detected also in reports of other Dionysiac myths and rituals . . ."

The question I think most helpful is this one: Why does the play make such an effort to skewer the wisdom of intellectuals? There are obvious passages from the chorus, and there is Pentheus' criticism of Dionysus; but there is also the bizarre treatment of Tiresias. Nothing in the tradition makes a sophist of Tiresias, or a butt of ridicule for that matter; in other plays he is an elderly and virtually omniscient diviner, and that is all. But in the *Bacchae* he leaves his traditional role behind and is ruthlessly parodied as a sophistical orator—except possibly for the last brief speech, in which he recovers some of his traditional dignity, if not his prowess as a diviner.[29] The most likely explanation is that Euripides has a bone to pick with the New Learning, and this is confirmed many times in the remainder of the play. Everything that anyone in the play sees as bad is associated with the New Learning. Cadmus' daughters think his advice to Semélê is a piece of educated cunning (line 30). Pentheus sees his adversary with eyes we know are diseased, because he is not an initiate, and he sees Dionysus in the early scenes first as a wizard and then as a sophist[30] (the roles were not widely separated in the minds of Athenians at the time); only when Pentheus sees the god as a bull is he beginning to see correctly (line 924). We in the audience share Pentheus' bad vision: Dionysus shows himself as a sophist to those who see his bad side. Most importantly, the chorus sees those who oppose them in Thebes entirely as an unholy alliance of ambition, innovation, and

---

(Seaford 1994, pp. 318–19). The main evidence is vase paintings, which are reproduced in LIMC (1981) and discussed by Dodds (1960, pp. xxxiii–xxxv; see also Seaford 1996, p. 27, n. 16). Beyond this, we would have had a better sense of Euripides' originality on specific points if Aeschylus' plays on Dionysus had survived, as Kirk points out (1979, p. 11).

29. Tiresias makes a more conventional appearance in Euripides' *Phoenician Women*, written not long before the *Bacchae*. There, at lines 865 ff., he makes use of no sophistic techniques, but delivers a straight prophecy that for once is believed, with tragic consequences: a boy takes his own life. In his familiar cameo roles in Sophocles' *Oedipus* and *Antigone* he speaks with authority derived from the gods, and is not believed. In the *Bacchae*, by contrast, he does not stand on his authority as a priest, makes no prophecies, and tries to make the most of human reason.

30. Pentheus sees Dionysus as a verbal trickster at 234, 475, 479, 489, 491, 650, 655, 801, and 824. Agavê sees the cunning sort of sophia in Dionysus at 1189–90.

clever sophistication parading falsely as wisdom.[31] Now this is entirely gratuitous: Pentheus is a naive young man clinging to traditional ideas and desperately afraid of innovations that would upset the balance of control men have over women. Pentheus is as disturbed by the New Learning as is the chorus. No Theban in the play represents the New Learning except Tiresias, and he is no threat to anyone.

Why then does the play repeatedly attack the New Learning? Euripides himself has been influenced by the movement, and this is well known by the Athenians, for Aristophanes has scored off the charge (note 4). But whatever Euripides believed in his youth, when he comes to write the *Bacchae* he is evidently angry at the New Learning, for he seems to be tacking onto the play a message that does not appear to be integral to the plot. Perhaps he attacks the New Learning because he now sees it as a seductive trend that has led Athens into one disaster after another. Perhaps the matter is more personal, and he believes, from the perspective of advancing age, that the movement has somehow betrayed him. The wisdom of old age, after all, is like the wisdom of initiation—calm, accepting, and based on a sequence of experiences. It is not at all like the brilliant techniques of argument and persuasion that can be taught to the young to further their ambitions. Whatever else Euripides loved or respected in Dionysus-worship, the evidence of the chorus, so resonant and deeply felt, is that the playwright knew the joy of initiatory knowledge.[32]

Initiation occurs in many cults, but is especially appropriate in the case of Dionysus, the god who has a gift for combining opposites. It is not merely that he is gracious to his votaries and cruel to his enemies; that is said of many gods. Dionysus is a god who takes human form, a powerful male who looks soft and feminine, a native of Thebes who dresses as a foreigner. His parentage is mixed between divine and human; he is and is not a citizen of Thebes; his power has both feminine and masculine aspects. He does not merely cross boundaries, he blurs and confounds them, makes nonsense of the lines between Greek and foreign, between female and male, between powerful and weak, between savage

---

31. The chorus inveighs against elements that are associated with the New Learning, at 387–89, 395–97, 891–911, 999, 1005.

32. Winnington-Ingram wisely suggests that in the end Dionysus' true nature is manifest only to the poet (1947, p. 164).

and civilized. He is the god of both tragedy and comedy, and in his presence the distinction between them falls away, as both comedy and tragedy are woven into this extraordinary play. Most disturbing of all, Dionysus blurs the lines between the magnificence of a god, the petty angers of a human being, and the savage power of a lion or wild bull.

We might say, then, that Dionysus appears mysterious because he *is* mysterious, because it is his special role to undermine the boundaries set by human culture. But Dionysus is not a god of mystery; he is the god of what is known as a mystery *religion*. Characters in the play are mystified by Dionysus because they are not initiated in his religion, and therefore do not have the clarity of vision that comes through the Bacchic experience. Generally, Greek gods present themselves obscurely to those who are not their favorites, and they blur the vision of those whom they wish to destroy. Dionysus carries this to an extreme in the myth dramatized by the *Bacchae*.

Initiation is a journey by way of symbolic death and rebirth, from darkness into light, indicating the passage from ignorance to joyful knowledge. The candidate is expected to resist, and is led by a guide through much of the journey. Initiation requires passive acceptance, then, and its clarity cannot be achieved by one's own active powers.

What the initiate comes to know about Dionysus is not his appearance. When Pentheus asks, "You say you saw the god clearly. What did he look like?" Dionysus in human form answers, "Whatever way he wanted. I had no control of that" (477–78). Initiates are beyond the level of appearances; they know Dionysus simply for the power that he is. The chorus is not aware that the young man they follow is actually their god in disguise; but that takes nothing away from their knowledge of the god. They know him well through their common experience of him in the practice of their religion.

If Dionysus is an enigma, he is one to which the chorus of Bacchae knows the answer—and so does the Athenian audience. We modern readers are left in ignorance, partly because of the secrecy surrounding the actual rituals of Dionysus-worship, and partly because even if we knew every detail, we would not have the clarity claimed by initiates because we cannot claim to have felt the god's presence.

The point of the play is not that we should be content with

mystery and give up our ambition for a clear understanding. It is a peculiarly modern error to prize the mystery or ambiguity of Dionysus for its own sake. The point, rather, is that clear understanding comes only by way of initiation, and not by active intellectual efforts. If a deity strikes you as mysterious, that is because you have not been initiated into his or her mysteries. The mystery will only deepen if you try to lead yourself to a solution.

The play keeps before us a running contrast between wisdom and cleverness, a contrast by which modern scholarship (as Nietzsche saw) would be on the wrong side. The chorus would pity or fear us modern scholars, if they could know us through a reversing time machine. Our hard-won knowledge would be mere cleverness in their eyes.

Bibliographical Note

The translation of the *Bacchae* in Seaford's edition (1997) is almost word for word and will carry the Greekless reader as close as possible to the Greek text; Kirk's and Esposito's translations have similar virtues (1970, repr. 1979). Among literary translations, C. K. Williams's is now the best (1990).

The *Bacchae* has attracted the finest scholars of the century as editors and commentators—Gilbert Murray, E. R. Dodds, G. S. Kirk, Albert Henrichs, and now Richard Seaford. Readers who wish to go into questions of text and interpretation should consult Seaford's commentary or the notes in Kirk's and Esposito's editions, all of which are accessible to Greekless readers. Those who know Greek should consult Dodds's commentary as well.

The most influential interpretation of the play is by Charles Segal (1982; expanded edition, 1997); his magisterial afterword to the 1997 edition—which readers should consult as a supplement to this bibliographical note—reviews recent scholarship on the *Bacchae*.

Among books about the *Bacchae*, R. P. Winnington-Ingram (1947, repr. 1969) stands out, although it now appears dated in some respects. Roux's commentary (in French, 1970) is valuable, as is Gilbert Murray's reading of the play (1918). Oranje (1984) is especially helpful on understanding Pentheus. Seaford's study of ritual (1994) is now essential reading for any scholar of the play, and Martha Nussbaum's introduction to the Williams translation should be required as well. Valdis Leinieks's recent book about the *Bacchae* (1996) challenges common scholarly opinion on a number of points. Stephen Esposito's edition (1998) contains much useful scholarly material, and this is supplemented by an excellent online companion to the *Bacchae* at the web site *http://www.pullins.com*. Albert Henrichs's many articles must now be the starting point for scholarly work on Dionysus.

Images of Dionysus and Pentheus are to be found in LIMC (1981). See also Carpenter (1997).

On Greek theater and its place in religious festivals, the classic study is by Pickard-Cambridge (3d edition, 1990). Readers interested in staging the play should be aware of the studies by Oliver Taplin (1978), Donald Mastronarde (1979), and J. Michael Walton (1987). J. Winkler and F. Zeitlin's book of essays by various hands, *Nothing to Do With Dionysus?* (1990) contains essential reading on Greek tragedy, as does P. E. Easterling's *Cambridge Companion to Greek Tragedy* (1997).

Full citations for these works are given at the end of this volume.

The Daughters of Cadmus

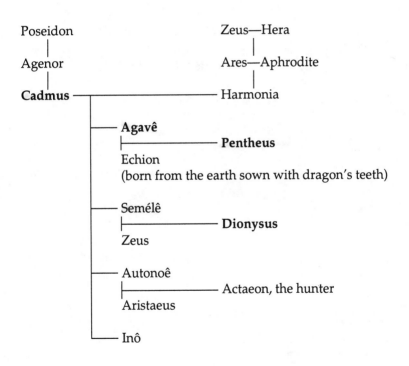

Poseidon

Agenor

Cadmus ——————————————————— Harmonia

Zeus—Hera

Ares—Aphrodite

Agavê

Echion
(born from the earth sown with dragon's teeth) —————— **Pentheus**

Semélê

Zeus —————— **Dionysus**

Autonoê

Aristaeus —————— Actaeon, the hunter

Inô

Cast of Characters

DIONYSUS   god of intoxication, son of the god Zeus and the
mortal Semélê, also known as Bacchus, Iacchus,
Evius, and Bromius

CHORUS   of Bacchae (also known as Maenads), the women
celebrants of Dionysus

TIRESIAS   a blind seer

CADMUS   founder and former king of Thebes, grandfather of
Dionysus and Pentheus

PENTHEUS   king of Thebes, cousin of Dionysus

AGAVÊ   daughter of Cadmus, mother of Pentheus

A SOLDIER IN PENTHEUS' ARMY

FIRST MESSENGER

SECOND MESSENGER

The *Bacchae* of Euripides

Prologue

DIONYSUS:

(dressed as a celebrant in his own religion)

I have arrived. I am Dionysus, son of Zeus,
come to Thebes, where my mother gave me birth
in a firestorm, struck by lightning. Her name
was Semélê; her father, Cadmus, had founded
this city. I have changed from divine to human form,   5
and here I am.

(pointing to various features of the landscape)

      There's the Ismenus River, the other one is called Dirkê.
Over here, by the house, is the marker for my mother's
  grave,
where she was struck by thunder. The ruins of her home
are still smoking from the living flame of Zeus. That
is how angry Hera was at my mother—violent, deathless
  rage.
                Cadmus, now, he's done well,   10
to keep this ground off limits, sacred to his daughter.
The vines that cover it, however, these are mine;
I set them around, made them copious and green.

My journey? I began from Lydia, where the sand is rich
15   in gold, then passed through Phrygia, then the sun-struck
plains of Persia, saw Bactria's walled towns, faced
the rigors of Media, and so came to rich Arabia. Then across
Asia, where fine-towered cities lie along the salt sea,
teeming with Greeks and other peoples mixed.
20   I came here—my first Greek city—
only after I had started initiations there
and set those places dancing, so that mortals
would see me clearly as divine. Now Thebes
is my choice to be the first place I have filled
25   with cries of ecstasy, clothed with fawnskin, put thyrsus
in hand—this ivy-covered spear—because my mother's
sisters—of all people, *they* should have known better—
said Dionysus was no son of Zeus. They said
Semélê was seduced by some man or other and
30   put the blame on Zeus (as Cadmus cunningly advised her)
for her mistake in bed, and Zeus killed her—they yawped
everywhere—because she pretended to be his wife.

That is why I have stung these women into madness, goaded
them outdoors, made them live in the mountain, struck
35   out of their wits, forced to wear my cult's panoply.
All the females, all the women of Thebes—I sent them
crazy from their homes. Even the king's daughters are
     running
wild with them under fir trees, or seated on rocks in the
     open.
This city must fully learn its lesson, like it
40   or not, since it is not initiated in my religion.
Besides, I must defend my mother, Semélê,
and make people see I am a god, born by her to Zeus.

Well, now, Cadmus has given his rights as king
to Pentheus, the son of his daughter Agavê,
45   and Pentheus wages war on the gods through me,
shoves me away from libations, pays no attention

21: Initiations—the core of Dionysus-worship as represented in this play
is an experience of initiation that leads, among other things, to a clarity of
vision in matters relating to the god; see Introduction, p. xli.

to me in his prayers. For that, I'll show him
I am truly god, and I'll show the Thebans too.
Then, once I've put this place in order, I'll
turn to another country, reveal myself there.   50
But if Thebes reacts in anger, sends military
force to drive my Bacchae from the mountain,
I'll lead my Maenads like an army into battle.
It's to do this that I have taken human form
and changed myself into a man.
Now come, my sacred band of women,   55
that came with me from the bulwark of Lydia,
Mt. Tmolus, companions in my journey from abroad.
Take up the drums, the native drums of Phrygia,
the ones I discovered, I and Mother Rhea.
Surround this royal home of Pentheus, and strike.   60
Make the city of Cadmus take notice. Meanwhile,
I'll join the Bacchae on the slopes of Mt. Kithairôn,
and take my part in their dances.

Choral Entry-song

(The chorus enters, responding to his call.)

CHORUS:
    Out of Asia
    from the sacred mountain, I hasten   65
    my sweet labor for the Thunderer
    I strain my voice—but it's no strain—
    shouting praise of Bacchus.

53: Maenads were women who celebrated Dionysus by dancing themselves into a frenzy on a mountainside, out of the sight of men.
57: Mt. Tmolus—famous for its gold-dust bearing rivers. Lydia and Phrygia are both in western Asia Minor (modern Turkey).
59: Rhea—a name for the mother goddess, whose worship was distinct from that of Dionysus.
62: Mt. Kithairôn—a mountain near Thebes. Maenads feel that the god is present in their rituals, although no human men are present. Dionysus proposes to join them, but probably not in human form.
66: Thunderer—Bromios, "the Roarer," a name for Dionysus.
68: Bacchus—another name for Dionysus.

You, on the road! You, on the road!
You, in the houses!
Come out! Let everyone
70   keep holy silence now.
For I shall sing the age-old hymn
to Dionysus.

[Strophe 1]

O
blessed are they
who know in their happiness
gods' initiations,
live life in holiness,
75   minds tuned to festival,
dancing on mountaintops,
sacred cleansing
in honor of Bacchus.

They celebrate the rites also
of the mother, great Cybélê
80   and they shake aloft their thyrsus
over heads enwreathed in ivy,
serving Dionysus.

Run, Bacchae! Run, Bacchae!
Bring the god, the son of a god,
85   Thunderer Dionysus,
down from the mountains of Phrygia,
down to Greece, to broad avenues,
Bromius.

[Antistrophe 1]

Born
suddenly in labor

73: A strophe is a large metrical unit, which is matched by its antistrophe.
74: Initiations—see Introduction, p. xli.
79: Cybélê is the mother goddess of Crete, whose worship—like that of Dionysus—involved dancing into a state of ecstasy.
83: Bacchae—the women celebrants of Dionysus, also known as Bacchants and, by outsiders, as Maenads.

pangs brought on by force:
Zeus' thunderbolt took wing,   90
struck him out the womb.
His mother lost her life
in the flash of lightning.

For a womb, Zeus took him
straight into the cavern of his thigh   95
and sewed him up secretly
with golden fasteners
to hide him from Hera.

He was born when, as the Fates
said, his time came: a god   100
with his bull's horns, and crowned
with his snake crown. That is why,
in their wild hair, the Maenads weave
    predator serpents.

[Strophe 2]

Oh, Thebes, Semélê's motherland,
may you be crowned in ivy,   106
and may you run green with creeping
vines, run fruitful and green.
Join the Bacchae, celebrate
with boughs of oak and fir.   110
Wear dappled fawnskins,
garland with locks of white
lamb's wool. And round your rebel stalks
weave holiness. Make haste: let all the land dance,
for now the Thunderer leads our revels.   115

To mountain! To mountain!
There waits a throng of women-born
now stung to leave their work
at loom and shuttle, stung by Dionysus.

98: As the wife of Zeus, Hera was hostile to the children he fathered with
other women.

[Antistrophe 2]

Oh, caverns of the band of youths,
120   sacred chambers that gave birth to Zeus
on Crete, where Corybants
thrice-crested in the caves, invented
125   this taut cowhide drum,
gave it the beat of a swift Bacchic dance
below flutes, sweet-wailing.
This was their gift to the Mother, to Rhea—
the drumbeat of Bacchic praise.

130   Then satyrs in ecstasy
brought it from the goddess mother
and set it to the dances
we celebrate in each third year,
a joy to Dionysus.

[Epode]

He gives delight on mountains
136   when from the festive throng he runs
clothed in sacred fawnskin, falls earthward,
hunts goat-kill blood, raw flesh-eating joy,
140   yearning for mountains in Phrygia, Lydia—
with Bromius in the lead.
VoHé
VoHé

It flows milk, the ground flows wine, it flows
the nectar of bees.

As smoke streams from incense
145   of Syria, Bacchus waves
his flaming torch aloft;

121: Corybants—the young men who protected the infant Zeus by bang-
ing drums and dancing. Dancing priests of Cybélê, called Corybantes,
were a novelty in Athens at the time of this play.
142: "VoHé"—the Bacchic joy-cry. Most translations print "euoi" or
"evehe," which look more like the Greek, but are not readily pronounce-
able in English.

he darts, he runs,
he dances, he puts
them on fire if they stray.
Shouting, he rouses them,   150
his long hair softly tossing to the sky,
and adds to their sweet cries his thundering call:
"Run, Bacchae! Run, Bacchae!
Rich from the gold-flow of Tmolus,
sing praise to Dionysus   155
over thundering drums
and cry VoHé
to the glory of the god
with shouts and Phrygian war-cries."   160

When the ebony flute, melodious
and sacred, plays the holy song
and thunderously incites the rush of women
    to mountain, to mountain,
then, in delight, like a colt with its mother   165
at pasture, she frolics, a lightfooted Bacchant.

Scene One

TIRESIAS:
Where's the gatekeeper? Call Cadmus to come out,   170
Agenor's son, who left his home in Sidon
and ringed this city of Thebes with towers.
Hurry up! Someone tell him Tiresias
wants him. He'll know why I'm here.
We made an agreement, he and I, to tie a thyrsus,   175
and—though I'm old and he's older—
to wear fawnskins and wreathe our heads in fresh ivy.

CADMUS:
Here you are, dear friend. I recognized your voice
from inside the house—such a wise voice, a wise man's
    voice.
And I'm ready. Look, I have my costume for the god.   180
As well I might. Considering he's my daughter's son
whom they've now discovered is a god, Dionysus,

we should build him up as best we can.
   Where should we go to dance? Where plant
185 our feet and toss our heads, gray as they are?
Be my guide in religion, Tiresias, the old leading
the old, since you're so wise. I hope I'm never tired
of rattling my thyrsus on the ground, night and day.
Isn't it delightful to forget how old we are?

TIRESIAS:
 I feel just the same as you:
190 I'm growing young, my feet want to dance.

CADMUS:
 So how shall we get to the mountain? By chariot?

TIRESIAS:
 No. That's no way to give honor to the god.

CADMUS:
 Then let me guide you as we walk, old as I am.

TIRESIAS:
 Don't worry. The god will lead us there—both of us.

CADMUS:
195 Are we the only men in Thebes who'll dance for Bacchus?

TIRESIAS:
 The only ones in our right minds. The rest are mad.

CADMUS:
 We're wasting time. Come, take my hand.

TIRESIAS:
 Of course. And you take mine: we'll be a team.

CADMUS:
 I'm not the one to look down on gods. I'm human.

TIRESIAS:
200 We don't try to be clever with the gods;
our traditions—which are old as time itself—

came from our forefathers. No sophistic arguments
will throw them down, no, not from the best brains of all.

CADMUS:
    Won't folks say I ought to be ashamed, taking up dancing
    now that I'm so old, and putting ivy on my head?   205

TIRESIAS:
    The god won't care who's young, who's old:
    we all must dance, because he wants
    honor from all of us, together. He'll not exclude
    anyone who gives to him the glory he desires.

CADMUS:
    Tiresias, I know you cannot see this shining light,   210
    so let me be your prophet and put it into words for you:
    Here's Pentheus coming home in a hurry—
    Echion's son, I made him king. My goodness,
    he *is* in a flutter. Strange! What do you suppose he'll say?

PENTHEUS:

    (addressing the audience)

    I happened to hear, when I was out of town,   215
    there's trouble in the city—a revolution:
    These women of ours have left their homes
    and run away to the dark mountains, pretending
    to be Bacchants. It's this brand-new god,
    Dionysus, whoever that is; they're dancing for *him!*   220
    They gather in throngs around full bowls
    of wine; then one by one they sneak away
    to lonely places where they sleep with men.
    Priestesses they call themselves! Maenads!
    It's Aphrodite they put first, not Bacchus.   225
    Those I've captured are chained by the hand,
    and they are under guard in public jail.
    As for the ones who got away, I'll hunt them

203: Some sophists taught people to use argument strategies like wrestling holds to throw their enemies; some also used arguments to undermine belief in the gods. See Introduction, p. xvi.
225: Aphrodite—goddess of love.

230   down out of the mountains—even my aunt
and my mother Agavê, and Actaeon's mother as well.
I'll catch them all in iron cages! I'll put a stop,
right now, to this dirty business, this Bacchism.
Also, I hear there's a foreigner come to town,
a wizard with magic spells from Lydia, who has

235   long blond curls—perfumed!—upon his head,
and the bloom of wine, the grace of Aphrodite,
on his cheeks. Day and night he plays around
with young girls, showing off his "VoHé"
mysteries. Just let me get him in this house!

240   I'll stop him rattling his thyrsus and shaking his hair,
once I have his head cut from his shoulders.
And *he's* the one who says Dionysus is a god,
that *he* was sewn up in the thigh of Zeus—
when actually he was burnt to ashes by lightning,

245   along with his mother, because she lied when she named
Zeus as her lover. That's a hanging offense, isn't it?
One insult after another. I don't care who he is . . .

      (catches sight of Tiresias and Cadmus)

What's this? Another marvel? Our expert reader
of omens in fancy fawnskins—is that you, Tiresias?

250   And my very own grandfather—what a laugh!—
playing Bacchant with a thyrsus. Shame on you, old man.
You both should have some sense at your age.
Why don't you shake that ivy off? And let
the thyrsus go, out of your hand, grandfather.

255   Tiresias, you talked him into this. You just want
to make a profit bringing in this new divinity so you
can check out more bird-omens and run more sacrifices.
If your gray hair hadn't stopped me, you'd be
sitting in chains surrounded by Bacchic women

260   for importing bad religion: because when women

230: Actaeon—son of Autonoê, grandson of Cadmus, and cousin of Pentheus and Dionysus, whose fate is frequently mentioned as parallel to that of Pentheus. He was torn apart by his own hunting dogs for an offense to the goddess Artemis. See lines 337 ff.

get their sparkle at a feast from wine,
I say the entire ritual is corrupt.

CHORUS LEADER:
Sacrilege! Friend, have you no respect for gods?
For Cadmus? Who planted the crop of earthborn men?
You are Echion's son: You'll disgrace your own family! 265

TIRESIAS:
When a prudent speaker takes up a noble cause,
he'll have no great trouble to speak well.
You, on the other hand, have a tongue that runs on smoothly
and sounds intelligent. But what it says is brainless.
True, boldness can help a man speak powerfully, 270
but he'll turn out bad for the city because he'll have no sense.
This "new divinity," the object of your ridicule,
has more greatness in his future here in Greece
than I can say. Young man, there are two
first principles in human life: the goddess Demeter 275
—or earth—you may use what name you like—
who nourishes us by means of the dry element;
and the second one balances her exactly, that's
Semélê's child, who discovered, in the wet element,
a drink from grapes, a drink he delivered to us. 280
This brings relief from pain for long-suffering mortals
when they are filled with the vineyard's bounty;
it grants sleep, lets them forget the evils of the day,
and there is no other cure for trouble.
We pour him out as libation to the gods, god that he is,
so that what good we have we have by way of him. 285
Now, do you think it's silly he was sewn in the thigh
of Zeus? I'll explain to you how fine this really was.
When Zeus had plucked him from the lightning fire
and raised the newborn to Olympus as a god,
Hera wanted to throw him down from heaven. 290
But Zeus contrived a defense worthy of a god:
he broke off a piece from the sky that circles the earth
and made a surrogate to give Hera as a hostage.
So that was how he saved the real Dionysus 293a

293: Hera evidently thought she had the real Dionysus, whom she kept as

from Hera's violent rage. After a while,
295   people began to say he'd been "sewn in thigh."
They put "sewn in thigh" for "showing sky" because
they heard that Zeus fooled Hera by "showing sky" to her.
Let me add, this god gives prophecy or foresight:
whatever is Bacchic—or maddened by his *force*—
300   has foresight aplenty, and when the god enters people
in force, he maddens them and makes them tell the future.
Also, he has his share of the war god's power, too:
Sometimes an army is in full gear, standing in order,
and they're struck by a panic before a weapon is touched.
305   That madness comes from Dionysus too.
Besides, you will come to see him on the crags of Delphi
with his torches, leaping on the twin-peaked mountain
shoulder, waving and shaking his Bacchic wand—
you'll see he's great everywhere in Greece.
                    Now, Pentheus, take my advice.
310   Do not brag about your power in controlling men;
and whatever your judgment should be, if it is ailing
do not judge that it is sound. Accept this god into your land;
pour him libations, join his Bacchic dance, put wreath on
        head.
It is not Dionysus who will force virtue on women
315   in matters of sex. You must look for this in their natures.
Even in a Bacchic revel, a woman who is really virtuous
will not be corrupted. Look. You are delighted
when the people crowd your palace gates
320   and the city resounds with the name of Pentheus.
In my opinion, it's the same with Dionysus—
he too is pleased by being honored. I, therefore,

---

a hostage for her husband's good behavior. But Zeus sent the real
Dionysus to be raised by nymphs in a place of safety. See endnote.
297: The pun in Greek is between *mêros* (thigh) and *homêros* (hostage).
Explanations based on word play or imagined derivations were common
in sophistic rhetoric of the period.
300: I have not been able to translate the Greek pun here; it is between
mania (frenzy) and *mantikê* (future-telling).
306: Prophecy is mainly the business of Apollo at Delphi; Tiresias is
suggesting that Dionysus has a share of Apollo's power, as well as that of
the war god Ares.

along with Cadmus—sneer at him if you will—
are wreathing our heads in ivy for the dance.
We are gray-haired, the pair of us, but still we must dance.
I'll make no war on gods; I do not accept your argument. 325
I am sorry to say it, but you are mad. Totally mad.
And no drug could help you, even though you're as sick
as if you had been drugged.

CHORUS LEADER:
Old man, Apollo's not insulted by your claims;
you are being sensible when you honor Dionysus,
great god that he is.

CADMUS:
Tiresias' advice is excellent, my boy. Stay home 330
with us, don't cross the threshold of the law.
You are flitting about, you know, so thoughtless,
the way you think.
    Suppose you're right, the fellow's not a god—
well, let him have the title anyway, as far as you care.
Tell a lie. It's a good cause: you'll make Semélê famous, 335
mother of a god. And our whole family reaps the glory.
Look what happened to Actaeon, your cousin—
he died horribly. His own dogs (he'd reared them himself
to eat raw meat) tore him in pieces, and all because
he bragged he was a better hunter in the mountains 340
than Artemis. Don't let that happen to you. Here,
put on this ivy. Join us. Let's give honor to the god.

PENTHEUS:
Keep your hands off me! Go ahead and be a Bacchant,
but don't you wipe that foolishness off on me.

    (pointing to Tiresias)

This "teacher" here infected you with silliness. 345
I will punish him.

331: Law—*nomos*, which can also mean "custom." Why does Cadmus
appeal to this in defense of a brand new religion? The chorus will do the
same (387, 891–96, and 995). See endnote on lines 891–96.

(turning to his guards)

                Send someone right away
to where he has his Seat of Divination.
Pry it up, turn it upside down, use levers,
and make a mess of the whole place. Take his sacred
350   head-wrappings and toss them out, leave them to
the wind and rain. I can't hurt him any worse than that.
You others, sweep the city. Track down that foreigner,
the one who looks like a girl. He carried this new disease
to our women, put this filth in our bedrooms.
355   If you catch him, bring him here in chains
so he can pay the penalty—death by stoning—and learn
what a serious crime it is to play Bacchus in Thebes.

TIRESIAS:
    Abomination! You haven't the faintest idea what you are
       saying!
    You've become a complete lunatic; this is no temporary
       madness.
360   Let's be on our way, Cadmus. We must win over the god
    with prayers—for this man's sake, violent as he is,
    and for the city's too. Otherwise the god may take
    a terrible revenge. Come with me, on your ivy-covered staff.
    Try to keep me upright, and I'll do the same for you.
365   It would be a shameful sight for two old men to fall. Still,
    we have to go, bow down to Bacchus as the son of Zeus.
    Pentheus' name means "grief"; I hope he brings no grief
    upon your family. This is not fortune-telling—
    I'm looking at facts: he who speaks foolishness is a fool.

FIRST CHORUS:

[Strophe 1]

370   O Reverence, queen of gods,
    Reverence, who over earth
    spread golden wing,
    Have you heard Pentheus?
    Have you heard the outrage,
375   insult to Thunderer
    son of Semélê—he who is first

of all the blessed powers
for joy at festivals
where heads are wreathed?
       His domain
is sacred dances
laughter by flutesong   *380*
relaxation of care,
whenever grapes shine
on feasting of gods,
or when, at ivy-wreathed festivals,
sleep steals round men from the wine bowl.   *385*

[Antistrophe 1]

Mouths that run unchecked,
lawless and senseless,
end in disaster.
But a life lived in peace   *390*
with good sense holds
family together,
stays unshaken.
Far away, the sky dwellers,
heavenly powers, may be;
but they are watching us.
Wisdom? It's not wise   *395*
to lift our thoughts too high;
we are human, and our time is short.
A man who aims at greatness
will not live to own what he has now.
That, I believe, is the life of men   *400*
whose judgment is foul.
       They are insane.

[Strophe 2]

Oh let me be in Cyprus,
Aphrodite's land,
where cupids dwell   *405*
and cast their spells upon our minds,
and where the river of a hundred mouths
makes rainless Paphos fruitful,

with water from afar.
410   Or there, on the sacred slope of Mt. Olympus,
lovely Pieria, home of the Muses—
Take me there, Thunderer, Thunderer,
leading spirit of the joyful cry,
to the land of the Graces,
415   the land of Yearning, the land where Bacchic
revels are the law.

[Antistrophe 2]

Divine, son of Zeus,
he rejoices in feasting,
he loves Peace the blissgiver,
420   cherisher of young men, goddess.
To rich and poor alike
he grants delight of wine
without pain.
And he hates the man who does not try—
425   each day, each longed-for night—
to live a flawless life
and wisely steers away,
in heart and mind,
from men who stand out above others.
430   What is ordinary,
what the crowd thinks right,
is good enough for me.

Scene Two

SOLDIER:
Pentheus, we are here. Mission accomplished.
We have hunted down this wild thing
435   you sent for, but we found the beast was gentle,
made no attempt to escape, willingly held out
its hands, did not turn pale or lose its blush of wine.
Instead, he laughed and had us take him prisoner.
440   He waited and made my task an easy one.

409: The river is the Nile, which was thought to issue in springs at Paphos,
on the island of Cyprus.

I was ashamed. I said, "This isn't my idea, Stranger.
Pentheus sent me under orders to capture you."
Now, about these Bacchic women you'd arrested,
chained, and locked up in the public jail—
they're free, they escaped to the mountains,   445
they're dancing around up there, calling on the god.
The chains simply fell off their feet, all by themselves,
and the doors—no human hand touched them,
but they were unlocked. So many miracles this man
has brought to Thebes! Well, the rest is your concern.   450

PENTHEUS:
You may release his hands. He's in my net; he won't
escape me now, no matter how quick he is.

   (looking him over)

Well, well. Not bad. You're actually quite good-looking.
I mean, to women. Of course, that's why you came to Thebes.
This long hair of yours—you're no wrestler, are you—   455
these curls along your cheek—oh, they'll swoon for you—
and this fine complexion—you had to work on that,
staying out of the sun, in the shadows, hunting,
with your pretty face, for sex, Aphrodite's business.

So tell me this first. Where are you from?   460

DIONYSUS:
Right away, sir. It's a simple story.
No doubt you've heard of Mt. Tmolus, where flowers grow?

PENTHEUS:
I have. Runs round the city of Sardis, circles it.

DIONYSUS:
That's where I'm from. Lydia is my country.

PENTHEUS:
What was your reason for bringing this cult religion to
   Greece?   465

463: Sardis is the capital of Lydia in western Asia Minor.

DIONYSUS:
> Dionysus made me an initiate himself, and he's a son of
> Zeus.

PENTHEUS:
> What do you have there—some Zeus who spawns new gods?

DIONYSUS:
> No. It was here he joined Semélê in marriage.

PENTHEUS:
> Did he take you by force in a dream, or did you see him?

DIONYSUS:
470 Face to face. And he personally taught me the rituals.

PENTHEUS:
> Tell me about these rituals. What do they look like?

DIONYSUS:
> They may not be revealed to those who are not Bacchants.

PENTHEUS:
> What's the good of these rituals to people who celebrate
> them?

DIONYSUS:
> Hearing that is forbidden you, but knowing it would be of
> value.

PENTHEUS:
475 What a neat quibble. Now I really want to hear.

DIONYSUS:
> Keep up that irreverence and the dance will turn hostile.

PENTHEUS:
> Now, you say you saw the god clearly. What did he look like?

DIONYSUS:
> Whatever way he wanted. I had no control of that.

PENTHEUS:
> Another clever diversion! You didn't say a thing.

DIONYSUS:
Speak wisdom to a fool and he'll think you have no sense at
all.   480

PENTHEUS:
Are we the first to whom you've brought this divinity of
yours?

DIONYSUS:
Outside Greece, everyone is already dancing for him.

PENTHEUS:
That's because foreigners have so little sense compared to us.

DIONYSUS:
In this case more, much more. They just have different
customs.

PENTHEUS:
You practice this cult by night or by day?   485

DIONYSUS:
Mostly at night. Darkness lends solemnity.

PENTHEUS:
Darkness is just a filthy trap for women.

DIONYSUS:
Some people can dig up dirt in daytime too.

PENTHEUS:
You'll have to be punished for this—this wicked cleverness.

DIONYSUS:
And you for stupidity, for irreverence to the god.   490

PENTHEUS:
Tough talk for a Bacchant! You get lots of exercise . . . with
words.

DIONYSUS:
What penalty do you propose? What horrible thing will you
do to me?

PENTHEUS:
  Let's start by shearing off your pretty goldilocks.

DIONYSUS:
  That's sacred! I grow my hair in honor of the god.

PENTHEUS:
  Next, hand over your thyrsus.

DIONYSUS:
495   Take it away yourself. The one I carry belongs to Dionysus

PENTHEUS:
  And we'll lock you up and keep you under guard.

DIONYSUS:
  The god himself will set me free, whenever I want.

PENTHEUS:
  Sure he will, whenever you stand among your Bacchae and
    summon him.

DIONYSUS:
500   Even now he's very near, and he sees what I am suffering.

PENTHEUS:
  Then where is he? He hasn't revealed himself to me.

DIONYSUS:
  He is where I am. You do not see him because you lack
    reverence.

PENTHEUS:
  Grab him! He has insulted me—and Thebes.

DIONYSUS:
  I proclaim: do not tie me. Believe me, I am sane and you are
    crazy.

PENTHEUS:
505   But I say, tie him up. Believe me, I have you in my power.

493: Growing long hair as a dedication to a god and later cutting it as a
religious offering had been common practice among men in ancient
Greece.

DIONYSUS:
    How do you live? What are you doing? Who are you? You
    don't know!

PENTHEUS:
    I am Pentheus, son of Agavê. My father was Echion.

DIONYSUS:
    Misfortune becomes you, with a name like that.

PENTHEUS:
    Get out! Lock him up over there in the horse-stalls.
    Let him stare at gloom and darkness.   *510*
    There's a place for you to dance.

        (Chorus starts to beat the drum.)

                    These women you brought—
    they're as guilty as you. We'll sell them as slaves,
    or I'll keep them myself, make them work at the looms.
    Either way, I will stop that damn noise.

DIONYSUS:
    I am prepared to go. Mind you, what cannot happen   *515*
    cannot injure me. But you! Dionysus will punish
    you for these insults, and you say he does not exist!
    When you abuse us, you are trying to put *him* in chains.

SECOND CHORUS:

                    [Strophe 1]

    Fair-maidened River Dirkê, queen
    of waters, daughter of Achélous,   *520*
    you who bathed
    the infant child of god—
    when Zeus the father pulled him,
    from undying fire, into his thigh,

508: Pentheus' name and misfortune—the Greek word for grief is *penthos*.
See line 1244.
520: The Achélous, the largest river in Greece, has no geographical link to
the smaller Dirkê River of Thebes, but stands here for all flowing waters.

525   did you not hear the cry of Zeus?

"Go, twice-born Dithyrambus,
into my male womb.
I now reveal you,
with your Bacchic name, to Thebes."

530   But now, blessed Dirkê,
you cast me out when I bring
wreaths and feasting to your shore.
Why do you reject me? Why do you run from me?
A time will come—I swear by all the joy
535   that you may squeeze from Dionysus'
grapes—a time when you *will*
pay attention to the Thunderer.

[Antistrophe 1]

What anger, oh what anger
shows now from the earthborn
spawn of a serpent,
540   Pentheus, begot
by Echion, the earthborn—
a wild-eyed monster
without a human face who
like a deadly giant wrestles with the gods!
545   Soon he will have me in his snares,
although I belong to the Thunderer.
Already he has my comrade in the sacred dance
imprisoned at home,
hidden in darkness.

550   Do you see this, son of Zeus,
Dionysus? Those who speak for you
are bound by force.
Come down from Olympus

526: Dithyrambus—a name for Bacchus.
539: According to the myth of Thebes' origin, Cadmus peopled his city by
sowing the teeth of a serpent he had slain, and from them sprouted men
to be his army.
544: The Olympian gods had, according to the myth, secured their power
by defeating a race of earthborn giants with the help of Herakles.

waving your gold-faced wand
and put down the insults of this deadly man. 555

[Epode]

Where are you now, Dionysus, waving your thyrsus?
Where on Nysa are you leading the dance,
on the mountain that feeds wild things?
Where? On the Corycian Peaks?
Perhaps at rest on Mt. Olympus, 560
in the wooded glades where Orpheus,
once upon a time, struck movement
into trees, and wild beasts, too,
followed the music of his cithara.

You are the blessed place, Pieria. 565
You are honored by the god of joyful cries.
He comes to set you dancing in his worship.
He will cross swift-flowing
rivers with his Maenads
whirling in their dance—the River Axion 570
and Lydias, father of waters,
who gives happiness and wealth to men
from the most beautiful flow of water
(so I have heard), for it fattens
the land with fine horses. 575

Scene Three

Dionysus:

(calling from offstage in his own voice, as a god)

Iô!
Hear me, hear my call!
Iô Bacchae, Iô Bacchae!

559: Nysa is probably a mythical mountain; Mt. Parnassus, with its Corycian Peaks, is near Delphi.
565: Pieria, on the slope of Mt. Olympus.
566: "The god of joyful cries"—Evius, from the cult-cry represented as VoHé.
571: The Axion and Lydias rivers are in Macedon.

HALF-CHORUS 1:
>   What's this? Oh, what? Where does it come from,
>   this roar of the joy-god, summoning me?

DIONYSUS:
580   Iô, Iô, I call again,
>   son of Semélê, son of Zeus.

HALF-CHORUS 2:
>   Iô, Iô, master, master!
>   Come to our sacred dance,
>   Thunderer, Thunderer!

DIONYSUS:
585   Queen of commotion, shake the earth's foundations!

HALF-CHORUS 1:
>   Ah! Ah!
>   Now the house of Pentheus will rattle down in ruins.

HALF-CHORUS 2:
>   Dionysus rises in the house!
>   Worship him!

HALF-CHORUS 1:
590   We worship. Oh, yes!

HALF-CHORUS 2:
>   Do you see? The stone crosspieces—
>   they're sliding off the columns!
>   The Thunderer!
>   He's raising Bacchic cries within the roofs.

DIONYSUS:
>   Strike, lightning bolt, brightly!
595   Burn the house of Pentheus,
>   burn it to ashes!

HALF-CHORUS 1:
>   Ah! Ah!
>   Look at the fire! Do you see how dazzling it is,
>   by the tomb of Semélê?

Where she, in former days,
left the flame of Zeus, thunderstruck?

HALF-CHORUS 2:
Fall to the ground, you trembling   600
Maenads, fall. For the lord
comes, he will cast this house
down to the dust. He is son of Zeus!

DIONYSUS:

(coming on stage in human form)

What frightened foreigners you women are
—down on the ground as if you had been struck!   605
Don't you see—it was Bacchus who shook the house apart?
Rise up, take courage, leave off trembling.

CHORUS LEADER:
It's you! Our great light in dancing to Bacchus!
How glad I am to see you! I was desolate, alone . . .

DIONYSUS:
Did you lose hope when I was sent inside?   610
Did you think I was trapped in Pentheus' dark jail?

CHORUS LEADER:
What else could I think? Who would protect me if you were
    lost?
But how did you get free from that unholy man?

DIONYSUS:
I saved myself. It was easy. No trouble.

CHORUS LEADER:
But I thought he tied your hands with knots of rope?   615

DIONYSUS:
There I made a fool of him. He thought he'd tied me up,
but he never laid a hand on me—he only fed himself on
    hope.
In the stable, where he planned to jail me, he came upon a
    bull,

620 and it was this he bound up, hoof and leg. He was panting
        fiercely
        as he tied the knots, biting his lips, sweat streaming down his
        body.
        I was very near; I sat peacefully and watched. That was when
        Bacchus came, shook down the house, and raised the flames
        over his mother's tomb. When the king caught sight of that,
625 he thought his house was on fire, ran up and down,
        told all his slaves to bring water from the river. What a waste
        of time! Then he let that job go because he thought I had
        escaped,
        so he grabbed his black sword and ran indoors. Now,
        the Thunderer—this is only how he appeared to me—I think
630 he formed an image of me in the courtyard for Pentheus
        to attack; he rushed up slicing clean air, trying to cut me
        down.
        Still Bacchus added outrage to outrage against him:
        shook the house down to the ground, totally ruined,
        so Pentheus could see what a painful mistake he had made,
635 putting me in jail. He's exhausted now, leans back
        and drops his sword—this man who dared do battle
        with a god! I left the house peacefully, and joined you here.
        Pentheus is nothing to me. But now—I hear his footsteps—
        he'll be here any minute. What will he say this time?
640 Well, never mind; even if he blows up a storm he will not
        bother me. A wise man trains his temper to be good and
        calm.

PENTHEUS:
        I've been tricked! It's horrible. That foreigner got away.
        The one I overpowered a few minutes ago and put in chains.
        Ah ha! There's the man!

        (to Dionysus)

645   What's this? What are you doing
        in the forecourt of my house? How did you get out?

DIONYSUS:
        Relax. Let peace lie firm beneath your anger.

PENTHEUS:
How did you break prison and get outside?

DIONYSUS:
Didn't you hear me? I told you Someone would set me free.

PENTHEUS:
Who? You keep saying strange new things. 650

DIONYSUS:
He who grows the clustering grapes for humankind—
that good deed, for which you held Dionysus to blame.

PENTHEUS:

(shouting to his soldiers)

Lock the gates! That's an order. Close off the city all around.

DIONYSUS:
What's the point? A god can leap over walls.

PENTHEUS:
What a wiseass you are—cunning, except where it counts. 655

DIONYSUS:
Where it counts the most, I was born cunning.

(He spies the messenger running down from the mountain.)

Wait.
You'd better listen to this man first. Pay attention.
He's bringing you news from the mountain.
We will wait, trust us, we will not run away.

FIRST MESSENGER:
Pentheus! Ruler of Thebes! I'm here from Mt. Kithairôn, 660
where white snow glistens, never failing.

PENTHEUS:
What's so important about the news you bring?

FIRST MESSENGER:
I saw the Bacchae in their sacred power, white

665   thighs shooting like arrows from the land.
      I'm here because I have to tell you—and the city, sir—
      what awe-inspiring things they do, beyond fantasy.
      But first I'd like to know whether you'll give me complete
      freedom to report what I saw there—or must I watch
670   my tongue? I am afraid of your quick temper, sir—
      so hot, so like a king, but too much.

PENTHEUS:
      Say anything. You'll be safe as far as I'm concerned.
      It's wrong to lash out at a law-abiding citizen.
      But for every horror you tell me about the Bacchae
675   I'll add to the sentence of punishment we'll give
      this person, for laying his clever schemes on women.

FIRST MESSENGER:
      Our herds of cattle climbed into the mountain
      meadow, just as the sun began to warm the earth.
680   And there I see them—three troops of women dancers,
      one led by Autonoê, the second by your mother Agavê,
      the third by Inô. They were all asleep, totally relaxed,

      some leaning back on pine boughs, others laid
685   their heads on oak leaves on the ground.
      They had let themselves go, in a sensible way,
      not as you said, sir, intoxicated by wine and flute,
      not running off by themselves in the woods for sex.

      Your mother leapt to her feet, wide awake
690   with a shout of ecstasy—Bacchae all around her—
      she'd heard the longhorns mooing.
      The others shook cozy sleep out of their eyes
      and sprang upright in close drill—an amazing sight—
      young and old, unmarried girls too.
695   First they let their hair down to their shoulders.
      and those who had loosened their fawnskin garments

      hitched them up and belted the spotted skins
      with snakes that licked their cheeks.
      Some of them cradled young gazelles or wolf cubs,
700   and gave white milk for them to suck.

695: Women in ancient Greece tied up their hair before sleeping.

These were ones who had just given birth,
and their breasts were swollen, their babies left behind.
All crowned themselves with ivy, oak and flowering
vines. One took her thyrsus, struck a rock,
and water leapt out, pure as dew.   705
Another set her staff in solid ground
and the god sent her a fountain of wine.
If anyone was thirsty for a drink of milk
she scrabbled her sharp fingers in the earth
and it came, spurting white. Sweet streams of honey   710
too came dripping from the ivy-covered wands.
And all in all, if you'd been there and seen these things
you'd come praying to the god whom you condemned.
Then we got together, cowherds and shepherds,
shared our stories, words clashing,   715
told each other the awe-inspiring things they did.
One man spoke up, a drifter who'd practiced
the art of words in town, "Hey, all of you who live up here
on the sacred mountain, wouldn't you like to hunt down
Agavê, yank Pentheus' mother out of her Bacchic dances,   720
and earn some favors from the king?" We thought
he'd spoken well, and so we laid an ambush,
hiding in the bushes. And they, at the appointed time,
spun into a Bacchic dance, shaking the thyrsus
and crying, "Iacchus," to the thunderborn child   725
of Zeus, all with one mouth, and the entire mountain
danced for Bacchus, wild beasts too, all racing into motion.

By chance, Agavê's leaping brought her next to me
and I sprang out—I meant to capture her—
and I gave up the ambush where we were hiding.   730
She raised a shout, "Oh you running dogs of mine,
these men are hunting *us!* Now follow me,
follow! A thyrsus is a weapon in your hands."
So we were the ones who ran away, to escape
being torn apart by Bacchae. And they attacked   735
our livestock as they were grazing on new grass.
No sharp weapons, but you'd have seen one woman
tear apart a young cow with her bare hands—
it was bellowing, its udder was swollen with milk. Others
ripped grown cows to pieces. You'd see ribs and feet   740

hurled every which way, hooves flying, pieces hanging
in the pine trees, smeared with blood and dripping.
Bulls in all their pride stumbled headlong:
They once had rage tossing on their long horns;
745   now more hands than you can count pull
them down—young girls' hands. And strip off the flesh
that covered them, faster than a king could wink one eye.
Then they took off like a flock of birds and raced
to the fields below, along the River Asôpus,
750   where Thebes grows bumper crops of grain.
Two villages, Hysiae and Erythrae, are settled there
beneath the heights of Mt. Kithairôn. And the Bacchae
fell on them like enemies on a rampage, tore
the towns to shreds, stole children from the houses,
755   put booty on their shoulders. (And even though
they did not tie it down, nothing fell to the dark earth
not bronze, not iron. And the fire they carried in their hair
never singed a curl.)

The village men were in a rage
at being plundered by the Bacchae; they grabbed weapons,
760   and then—sir, it was a terrible thing to see—
the men could not draw blood with their javelins,
but the women hurled the thyrsus and injured them
so badly they turned tail and ran—women over men!
only a god could make that happen.
765   Then they returned to where they had begun their dance,
to the springs the god had opened for them,
and washed off the blood, while the snakes licked
every drop clean from the skin of their cheeks.
This god, your majesty, whoever he is—
770   you'd better accept him for our city. He has great power
in other ways, but above all, I've heard it said
that he's the one who gives us wine to ease our pain.
If you take wine away, love will die, and
every other source of human joy will follow.

CHORUS LEADER:
775   I'm nervous about speaking freely to a king,
but even so, I have to say it:
No god is greater than Dionysus.

PENTHEUS:
This outrageous behavior of the Bacchae
is catching on like wildfire already. We'll be   ← *Ruled by women*
the laughingstock of Greece. No time for delay:
You, go to the south gate.   780
Call up our heavy infantry in their armor,
our cavalry, fleetfooted, and our light troops,
bearing small shields, the men
of singing bowstrings. Tell them all:
We will make war upon the Bacchae. This   785
is worse than anything—that the source
of so much trouble to us is women.

DIONYSUS:
You hear what I say, Pentheus, but you do not
take it to heart. Even though you've treated me badly,
I tell you, it's wrong to take up arms against a god.
Keep the peace. Dionysus will not stand for it if you drive   790
the Bacchae from mountains filled with cries of joy.

PENTHEUS:
Don't you lecture me! You just got out of your chains—
You don't like being free? Should I restore your penalty?

DIONYSUS:
Sooner than I'd suffer a pang of anger, if I were mortal
and he a god—I'd offer a sacrifice when he goads me.   795

PENTHEUS:
I'll make an offering—from the blood of women. They
deserve to die for raucous disturbances on Mt. Kithairôn.

DIONYSUS:
You will run away, all of you. You have tough bronze shields,
but you will be routed by the Bacchic thyrsus. What a
   disgrace!

PENTHEUS:
It's impossible to wrestle this foreigner to the ground!   800
Jail him or let him go, he keeps on talking.

795: Dionysus puns on the words for sacrifice and anger, which are close
in sound.

DIONYSUS:
Sir, there's still a way to make this come out well.

PENTHEUS:
Really? You want me to give in to my own women, my
slaves?

DIONYSUS:
I'll bring the women here—no weapons.

PENTHEUS:
The hell you will. It's another trick you've invented, against
805   me.

DIONYSUS:
Not at all. My only wish is to use my skill to save you.

PENTHEUS:
It's a plot! You've promised the Bacchae to keep up the dance
forever.

DIONYSUS:
Yes, I have promised, as you say . . . but to the god.

PENTHEUS:
Bring me my weapons! And you, shut your mouth.

DIONYSUS:
810   Wait.
Would you like to see the women gathered on the mountain?

PENTHEUS:
Of course. I'd give a pot of money for that.

DIONYSUS:
Really? Isn't this great passion of yours rather sudden?

PENTHEUS:
Well, it would hurt me to see them if they're drunk, but . . .

DIONYSUS:
815   Still, while you hated it, you'd enjoy the spectacle.

PENTHEUS:
Yes, of course, and I'd be quiet and sit under a pine tree.

DIONYSUS:
  They'll track you down, no matter how sneaky you are.

PENTHEUS:
  OK. I'll stay in the open. You give good advice!

DIONYSUS:
  Will I be leading you, then? And will you undertake this
    journey?

PENTHEUS:
  Yes, don't waste a minute. Lead on!   820

DIONYSUS:
  First, let's fit you out, cover your hide with a linen dress.

PENTHEUS:
  What? Change rank from man to woman?

DIONYSUS:
  They'll kill you if they see you as a man.

PENTHEUS:
  Good point, as before. You've been pretty cunning all along.

DIONYSUS:
  We owe it to Dionysus. He's our inspiration.   825

PENTHEUS:
  Good strategy. Now, how do we implement it?

DIONYSUS:
  Just step inside your house and I'll fit you out.

PENTHEUS:
  How? As a woman? That's disgusting!

DIONYSUS:
  Changed your mind? Don't want a view of the Maenads?

PENTHEUS:
  As for my outfit, what did you propose to cover me with?   830

DIONYSUS:
Start with your head. I'll give you a wig with long hair.

PENTHEUS:
And what next? Another decoration?

DIONYSUS:
A dress. Full-length. And a headband around your hair.

PENTHEUS:
Anything else you'd like to add?

DIONYSUS:
835   A thyrsus for your hand, and a spotted fawnskin.

PENTHEUS:
No. I couldn't put on a woman's outfit.

DIONYSUS:
But you'll cause bloodshed, if you attack the Bacchae directly.

PENTHEUS:
Right. Then I should go first to observe the situation.

DIONYSUS:
That's cunning. Otherwise, you'd use trouble as bait for
    trouble.

PENTHEUS:
840   But how can I sneak through the city without being seen?

DIONYSUS:
We'll use empty streets. I'll be in front.

PENTHEUS:
Most important: I don't want the Bacchae laughing at me.
Let's go inside—I'll make a decision.

DIONYSUS:
As you wish. My plan works either way.

842: laughing at me—that is, in triumph.

PENTHEUS:
   I will set out—either marching under arms   *845*
   or in the manner you advised.

      (Exit.)

DIONYSUS:
   That man! Women, he's on the edge of the net:
   His death will give justice, and he's coming to the Bacchae.
   Dionysus, the work is yours to do. I know you're very near.
   Pay him back. First, drive him out of his wits.   *850*
   Fill him with a skittish frenzy. He'll never want
   to take on a woman's dress in his right mind.
   But if he marches right outside his senses, he will get
      dressed.
   And I have a longing to see him jeered in Thebes,
   as he's led through the city looking like a woman—   *855*
   in return for those threats he made, trying
   to be formidable. Now I'm off to get the fine clothes
   I will fit to Pentheus for his trip to Hades when
   his mother kills him. Then he will know the son of Zeus,
   Dionysus, and realize that he was born a god, bringing   *860*
   terrors for initiation, and to the people, gentle grace.

THIRD CHORUS:

                        [Strophe]

   To dance the long night!
   Shall I ever set my white foot
   so, to worship Bacchus?
   Toss my neck to the dewy skies   *865*
   as a young fawn frisks
   in green delight of pasture?

   She has run away now from a fearful
   hunt, away from watchful eyes,
   above tight-woven nets—   *870*
   while the dogleader cheers
   the running of his hounds.

   She strains, she races, whirls and prances
   on meadows by rivers, delighting

875   in absence of men
         and under shadow-tresses
         the tender shoots of the wildwood.

                              [Refrain]

         What is wise? What is the finest gift
         that gods can give to mortals?
         A hand on the heads
880   of their enemies, pushing down?
         [No.] What is fine is loved always.

                              [Antistrophe]

         Never hurried, never
         failing, a god's
         fist comes down on men
885   who love to be hard-hearted,
         who hold back what is due to gods
         in the madness of bad judgment.
         Ingenious, how the gods
         keep time's long foot a secret
890   while hunting down irreverent men.
         No one should ever be above the law,
         neither in thought nor action.

         The cost of these beliefs is light:
         power lies
         with whatever thing should be divine,
895   with whatever law stands firm in time
         by nature ever-natural.

                              [Refrain]

         What is wise? What is the finest gift
         that gods can give to mortals?
         A hand on the heads
900   of their enemies, pushing down?
         [No.] What is fine is loved always.

881: [No]—This is how the chorus thinks the question should be an-
swered, but it is not explicit. See endnote.

[Epode]

Happy the man who has come away
safe on the beach from a storm at sea,
happy the man who has risen above
trouble and toil. Many are the ways   905
one man may surpass another
in wealth or power,
and beyond each hope there beckons another
hope without number.
Hope may lead a man to wealth,
hope may pass away;
but I admire a man when he   910
is happy in an ordinary life.

Scene Four

(Enter Dionysus.)

DIONYSUS:

You who long to see what is forbidden,
you who seek what must not be sought,
you, Pentheus, come out and let me see you here
before your house in a woman's gear, a Maenad's,   915
you spy against your mother and her troops.

(Enter Pentheus.)

Why, you look just like one of Cadmus' daughters!

PENTHEUS:

Hey, I think I am seeing two suns, I'm seeing double—
Thebes, the seven-mouthed fortress, all double.
And you're a bull, ahead of me in procession;   920
I see new horns sprouted on your head.
Were you ever a wild animal? You're being a bull now.

DIONYSUS:

The god is with us; he's not angry anymore.
He has made peace with us, and now you see things as you
    should.

PENTHEUS:

925   How do I look now? Is this the way Inô stands?
        Or my mother Agavê?

DIONYSUS:

        When I see you I think it's one of them.
        But this little curl of yours is out of position;
        it's not where I set it under your headband.

PENTHEUS:

930   I think I shook it up and down indoors, dancing
        like the Bacchae. That made it leave its post.

DIONYSUS:

        I'll put it back in order; that's my duty,
        to serve you. Hold your head straight.

PENTHEUS:

        Sure. You arrange it. I'm in your hands.

DIONYSUS:

935   Your sash is loose, your pleats are uneven,
        and your dress has slipped below your ankles.

PENTHEUS:

        I guess it has. But only on *this* side.
        Over here my dress hangs right.

DIONYSUS:

        You will surely think I am your closest friend when you see
940   how modestly the Bacchae dress—more so than you'd expect.

PENTHEUS:

        Should I hold my thyrsus this way, or in my right hand?
        I want to look like one of them.

DIONYSUS:

        Right hand. And lift it in time with your right foot.
        I'm delighted at your change of mind!

PENTHEUS:

945   Will I be strong enough to lift Mt. Kithairôn
        to my shoulders, Bacchae and all?

DIONYSUS:
> Yes, if you wish. Your mental state
> used to be unhealthy. Now it is as it should be.

PENTHEUS:
> Should we bring crowbars? Or do I barehanded
> thrust my arm or shoulder underneath the summit?   950

DIONYSUS:
> Mind you, you must not smash the Nymphs' temples
> or the places where Pan loves to play his pipes.

PENTHEUS:
> That's right. A strong fist is not what conquers
> women. I'll hide myself in the fir trees.

DIONYSUS:
> You'll find the hiding place a man should have   955
> if he goes to trick the Maenads as a spy.

PENTHEUS:
> Yes, I can imagine them like birds in a thicket,
> held in a sweet tangle of sex!

DIONYSUS:
> And that is why you're assigned guard duty.
> Perhaps you'll catch them . . . unless you're caught first.   960

PENTHEUS:
> Take me through the middle of Thebes.
> I am the only man in the city who dares to do this.

DIONYSUS:
> Only you. You bear the city's pain alone,
> and the contest you will face is meant for you.
> Follow me. I am your guide and your protection.   965
> Someone else will bring you back.

PENTHEUS:

> *(interrupting)*

> My mother!

DIONYSUS:
Everyone will be impressed . . .

PENTHEUS:

(interrupting)

That's why I'm going!

DIONYSUS:
You will be carried . . .

PENTHEUS:

(interrupting)

You'll spoil me!

DIONYSUS:
In your mother's arms.

PENTHEUS:
You'll pamper me to pieces.
You'll make me tender, by force.

DIONYSUS:
I will indeed.

PENTHEUS:
970   I will have what I deserve.

DIONYSUS:
You are wonderful and terrible; wonders and terrors await
    you
where you go. You will win glory towering high as heaven.

(Exit Pentheus.)

Now, Agavê, stretch out your arms,
and you too, her sisters, Cadmus' daughters.
975   I am bringing the boy for a great contest,
which I will win—I and Dionysus.

(Exit Dionysus.)

FOURTH CHORUS:

[Strophe]

Run, swift hounds of madness, run to mountain!
Find where Cadmus' daughters hold their celebration,
Sting them to fury at the man
who parties in a woman's outfit   980
and spies in madness on Maenads.

His mother will be first. She'll see him
on smooth rocks, or in a tree lurking.
She'll call the Maenads to her.

"Who is this   985
who longs for us, for the mountain-runners of Cadmus?
To mountain, to mountain, he came, he came!
Oh, Bacchae, who
could his mother have been? No women's blood in him;
he's a lion's whelp, or the cub of Gorgons from Libya."   990

[Refrain]

Now, Vengeance, out in the open!
Now, Swordbearer, slice through his throat!
He is godless, lawless, and unjust;   995
he is Echion's son, the earthborn.

[Antistrophe]

His judgment wrong, his feelings tuned against the law,
he can't abide your worship, Bacchus, or your mother's.
Intelligence gone mad,
spirit struck to arrogance, he has appointed   1000
himself to suppress the unconquerable by violence.

Death makes judgment sound, hears no
excuses. When you face the gods, remember
your mortality, if you'd live a painless life.

Wisdom you may have;   1005
I'd rather hunt for other virtues,
great ones and more plain: for a good life,
live reverently,

through night and day,
and if customs reach beyond justice,
1010   cast them out, and honor the gods.

[Refrain]

Now, Vengeance, out in the open!
Now, Swordbearer, slice through his throat!
1015   He is godless, lawless, and unjust;
he is Echion's son, the earthborn.

[Epode]

Be seen as a bull, be seen many-headed,
be seen as a serpent, or lion blazing fire.
1020   Bacchus, come with laughing face,
after the beast-catching man who hunts Bacchae;
tangle him in your fatal net, as he falls
beneath a pack of Maenads.

Scene Five

SECOND MESSENGER:
Oh, this house, this family! All Greece thought it lucky,
1025   once. That old man who came from Sidon, sowed
the earthborn crop from a serpent in the ground!
How I grieve for you! And I'm only a slave.

CHORUS LEADER:
What is it? What news from the Bacchae?

SECOND MESSENGER:
1030   Pentheus is dead, the child of Echion.

CHORUS LEADER:
Lord Bacchus! Great god revealed.

SECOND MESSENGER:
What are you saying? What did you mean? Woman,
you can't be happy over this calamity to my master?

CHORUS LEADER:
I'm a foreigner. I sing a hymn of praise that's strange

to you. Because I am free at last from the fear of prison. 1035

SECOND MESSENGER:
Do you think we are so unmanly here in Thebes
that we will not punish you for this?

CHORUS LEADER:
Dionysus! Dionysus holds me
in his power. Not Thebes.

SECOND MESSENGER:
I sympathize, but you women should not rejoice 1040
when evil has been done. It is not proper.

CHORUS LEADER:
Tell me, I want to know exactly how he died.
He was unjust, he was a fountain of injustice.

SECOND MESSENGER:
We left the outskirts of Thebes and crossed
the Asôpus River, then headed for the heights
of Mt. Kithairôn. Pentheus and I 1045
(I was following my master) and the foreign stranger
who was our guide on that observation patrol.

First we occupied a grassy hollow,
maintaining silence—walking carefully, no talking—
so that we could see without being seen. 1050
Between two cliffs, we spotted a ravine
laced with trickling streams, shaded by pines.
And there were the Maenads, sitting happily at work.
Some were rewinding ivy tendrils
around a thyrsus that had come undone; 1055
others, like colts set free from a decorated yoke,
tossed back and forth the singing of a Bacchic hymn.
Pentheus, poor man, could not see the whole crowd
of women. "Stranger," he said, "from where we stand

1037: A line with this meaning has evidently dropped out of the mss.
1056: decorated yoke—a symbol of marriage. See Introduction, p. xvi, on
the taming of animals, the control of women, and their reversal in this
play.

1060   my eyes can't reach as far as those phony Maenads.
        But if I climb some tower of a fir tree on the high ground
            there,
        I could accurately observe the Maenads' shocking behavior."

        Then I saw the stranger do something amazing.
        He grabbed a fir tree by its topmost shoot in the sky
1065   and pulled it down, down, down, to the black earth,
        bent like a bow or like a round wheel
        when the compass scribes its running arc.
        That's how he pulled down the mountain tree,
        and bent it to the earth. No mere human could have done it.
1070   He seated Pentheus in the fir branches
        and let the trunk go straight, gently easing up
        with his hands, careful not to shake him off.
        The tree towered straight up in the air
        with my master seated on its back.
1075   But they saw him, better than he saw the Maenads.
        Just before he came into view, sitting on high,
        the stranger disappeared altogether, and out of the sky
        came a voice—it must have been Dionysus,
        shouting to rouse the young women:
        "I have brought him to you, girls—the one
1080   who ridiculed me and my worship.
        Now you must pay him back."
        And with this pronouncement came
        sacred fire, linking heaven and earth.
        Then, silence in the sky, and silently the wooded glen
1085   restrained its leaves, wild creatures gave no cries.
        The women did not know what sound they'd heard;
        they stood stock still and cast their eyes about.
        Again, he gave command. Then Cadmus' daughters
        knew surely this was a command from Bacchus,
1090   and they ran with the speed of a dove;
        the Bacchae followed, darting down the ravine
        past jagged rocks and snow-melt torrents, while the god
1095   breathed madness in them. When they saw my master
        sitting in the fir-tree they started to throw slingstones
        up at him with great force; some climbed a facing
        pinnacle of rock and hurled fir-boughs like javelins.
        Others made missiles of the thyrsus and let

fly at Pentheus—a cruel volley, but it fell short. 1100
He was higher than their zeal could reach, up
there on his miserable seat, caught with no defenses.
In the end they struck at his tree roots with thunder-
bolts of oak branches, trying to pry them up. But those
were no iron crowbars, and their efforts led nowhere. 1105
So Agavê said, "Come on, stand in a circle, Maenads,
and grab the trunk. Let's catch this tree-mounting
beast; and keep him from telling the world
the secret of our dances to the god. Thousands of hands
took the fir-tree and plucked it right out of the earth. 1110
And he fell, ground-plummeting, from on high,
his high perch, wailing all the way down.
That was when Pentheus learned he was near to disaster.
His mother was the first at the killing. She was priestess,
and she rushed to attack him. He tore off his headband 1115
in hopes she would recognize him, not kill him.
He reached out to her cheek, miserable Agavê's,
and said, "I am yours, Mother, your child Pentheus.
You gave me birth in the house of Echion.
Pity me, Mother. I have made mistakes. 1120
But do not kill your own son because of them."
She was foaming at the mouth, face twisted, eyes
rolling, not thinking as she ought to think. She
was possessed by Bacchus and did not believe him.
Grabbing his left wrist with her hands, she braced 1125
her foot against his ribs—what a horrible fate for him—
and tore off his shoulder—but not by brute strength.
The god made it come off easily in her hands.
On the other side Inô was taking him apart,
breaking off bits of meat. Autonoê and the mob of Bacchae 1130
all went after him then. Then there was screaming
  everywhere.
He kept crying in pain as long as he had breath; they
were howling in triumph. Off went one with a forearm,
another took his foot—with its hunting boot. And his ribs
were stripped, flesh torn away. They all had blood on their 1135
hands. They tossed Pentheus' meat like balls in a game of
  catch.
The body is spread around: one piece by a rugged
cliff, another deep in the woods under heavy foliage,

impossible to find. His head—this is horrible—
1140   it turned out that his mother took it in her hands.
        She's got it planted on the tip of her thyrsus,
        and she's carrying it straight down Kithairôn (thinks
        it's a mountain lion's), leaves her sisters to dance
        for Bacchus. She's gleeful about her hunting (her luck
1145   was cruel). She's inside the walls now, shouting
        and praising Bacchus: "My hunting partner," she calls him,
        "who helped me run the dogs and catch my prey!
        Glorious victory!" (But all she's won is tears.)
                        I'm going now, before Agavê reaches home.
        I won't be underfoot when there's a disaster.
        But this is the highest glory: have a sound mind and
1150   reverence for
        whatever belongs to gods. This too is the most wise
        of all pursuits a human being can follow.

FIFTH CHORUS:
        Strike up the dance for Bacchus,
        raise a cheer for the downfall
1155   of serpent-spawn Pentheus,
        who fitted himself out as a woman,
        took for a thyrsus the staff
        that promises Hades,
        and paraded after a bull—to his downfall.

1160   Bacchae of Cadmus,
        your glory-song turns to a dirge, your fame to tears
        —a fine contest, to end with blood streaming
        from a hand thrust
        against a child.

CHORUS LEADER:
1165   Now I see her, she rushes home eagerly—
        Pentheus' mother, Agavê. Her eyes are rolling
        wildly. Welcome her, as a band of Bacchic revelers.

Exodos (Final Scene)

*(Enter Agavê, with the head of Pentheus on a stick, his hair
curled round it like ivy on a thyrsus. She enters immediately*

into the rhythms of the chorus and soon becomes part of their dance.)

AGAVÊ:
Bacchae from Asia!

CHORUS LEADER:
What are you shouting about?

AGAVÊ:
We're bringing it home from the mountains, 1170
a fresh-cut curling
shoot of the vine. Our hunting was blessed.

CHORUS:
I see. Come, you are one of us.

AGAVÊ:
I caught him, with no ropes or snares.
A lion's cub—
he's young, can you see? 1175

CHORUS:
From a wild place! Where?

AGAVÊ:
Kithairôn.

CHORUS:
Kithairôn?

AGAVÊ:
Slaughtered him!

CHORUS:
And the first blow? Whose was it?

AGAVÊ:
Mine. It was my privilege.
The sacred dancers call me "Blessed Agavê." 1180

CHORUS:
Who else?

AGAVÊ:

Cadmus . . .

CHORUS:
Cadmus?

AGAVÊ:

His daughters.
They got to the beast after I did, after me.
Oh, we had such luck in our hunting.

(*Here the lyric rhythm of the piece begins to repeat the pattern
set at Agavê's entrance.*)

AGAVÊ:
So join me in the feast.

CHORUS:

What feast? Join you? In misery?

AGAVÊ:
1185 He's young. The young bull just begins
to grow curls down his cheeks
and the hair on his head is soft.

CHORUS:
His hair, at least, would suit a beast from the countryside.

AGAVÊ:
Bacchus, dogdriving hunter, was cunning.
1190 Cunningly he roused Maenads
against this beast.

CHORUS:
The lord is a hunter!

AGAVÊ:
You praise?

CHORUS:

I praise

AGAVÊ:
Soon Cadmus' people . . .

CHORUS:
> and your son Pentheus . . .

AGAVÊ:
He'll praise his mother
for catching this big game, this lion's cub.   *1195*

CHORUS:
Outstanding catch!

AGAVÊ:
> Outstanding hunt!

CHORUS:
Do you rejoice?

AGAVÊ:
> I exult!
It was magnificent, magnificent,
what the hunt achieved, for all to see.

CHORUS:
Then show it to the city people now, wretched woman.   *1200*
Show them your victory—the game you brought from the
> hunt.

AGAVÊ:
Come, all you who dwell in the fine-walled city
of Thebes! Come and look at the big game
we daughters of Cadmus chased and caught.
We didn't need any throw-strap javelins   *1205*
or even nets. We used our own white arms,
just the fingers on our hands. We have made
spearthrowing obsolete, put weaponmakers out
of business. With hands alone we caught
this beast and tore it limb from limb.   *1210*

Where's my father, the old man? I want him
here. And Pentheus, my son—where is he? I want him
to take a great strong ladder and lean it on the house
so he can nail this to the beam-ends, now that I've
come with the head of a lion I hunted down.   *1215*

1215: Heads of sacrificial victims and possibly of game were hung high on
buildings.

(Enter Cadmus, followed by servants carrying the remains of Pentheus covered on a stretcher.)

CADMUS:
>   This way. That horrible thing you carry
>   is Pentheus. This way, in front of the house.
>   It took me endless trouble to find the body
>   in the ravines of Kithairôn and bring it here,
> 1220 all torn apart, no two pieces in the same place.
>   It was very hard to find them in the woods.
>   I didn't hear from anyone what my daughters had done—
>   the reckless maniacs!—till I was back in the city
>   after coming down from the Bacchic dance
> 1225 with old Tiresias. So I hurried back to the mountain
>   and here I am, bringing the boy who was killed
>   by Maenads. I saw Autonoê up there—that was
>   Actaeon's mother—and Inô too, still afflicted,
>   raving in oak-thickets, bitten with frenzy. But Agavê—
> 1230 someone said she'd danced her way down here
>   in Bacchic style, and it's quite true what I heard.
>   I am looking at her now, and what a miserable sight she is!

AGAVÊ:
>   Father, no one can brag about his daughters more
>   than you; we are the best daughters a man could have,
> 1235 by far. All of us, but me especially.
>   I gave up weaving, left my shuttles beside the loom,
>   turned to more important work—big-game hunting,
>   barehanded. And I brought you this with my own arms—
>   Do you see? It's the hero-trophy I captured,
> 1240 so you could hang it on your house. Take it,
>   Father. Put out your hands. Show off my success
>   at hunting to your friends, announce a banquet.
>   You are blessed, blessed! We have achieved such things!

CADMUS:
>   Grief beyond measure—I can't take it in.
> 1245 Achieved? Wretched hands! It's murder.
>   A fine victim for a sacrifice! You strike him down for the
>   gods

1244–45: Most editors delete these lines.

and then invite all Thebes and me to the feast!
Oh, I grieve more for your disaster than for mine.
The god had a right to destroy us, this lord of thunder.
But he went too far, considering he was born in our family. 1250

AGAVÊ:
Well, you're hard to please! That's old age for you,
always puts a scowl in a man's eye. I wish my son
would follow my example, and be a lucky hunter
whenever he goes after game with the boys
from Thebes. But all he can do is wage war 1255
on gods. He needs you to give him a piece
of your mind, Father. Who will call him
into my sight, so he can see me in my good fortune?

CADMUS:

   (crying in horror)

When you know what you've done,
you'll feel the most terrible agony of pain. But if you stay 1260
in the state you're in forever, you'll be
unlucky to the end, and never have the faintest idea.

AGAVÊ:
What do you mean? It's not beautiful? It's painful?

CADMUS:
First let your eyes look at the sky. Up here.

AGAVÊ:
I'm looking. Why did you suggest I look at this? 1265

CADMUS:
Is it the same? Or do you think it changes?

AGAVÊ:
It's brighter than before, a new glow comes through it.

CADMUS:
And that fluttering sensation, still have that in your soul?

AGAVÊ:
I don't know what you mean. But I am somehow coming
back into my mind, I'm moving away from the old thoughts. 1270

CADMUS:
Can you listen now and answer clearly?

AGAVÊ:
I've forgotten what we were saying, Father.

CADMUS:
When you married, what house did you go to?

AGAVÊ:
You gave me to Echion—a Sown Man. So they say.

CADMUS:
1275   And who was the son born at home to your husband?

AGAVÊ:
Pentheus, from my marriage to his father.

CADMUS:
Tell me, now. Whose face do you have in your arms?

AGAVÊ:
A lion's. At least that's what they said, the hunters.

CADMUS:
Look straight this time. It won't take long to see it.

AGAVÊ:
1280   Oh! What am I looking at? What am I carrying in my arms?

CADMUS:
Look carefully, and you will learn the answer clearly.

AGAVÊ:
I see horrible pain. I am so miserable.

CADMUS:
You don't think it looks like a lion anymore?

AGAVÊ:
No. It's Pentheus. I have his head.

1274: Sown Man—grown from a serpent's tooth planted in the ground
(see note for line 539).

CADMUS:
We mourned for him before you even knew who he was.   *1285*

AGAVÊ:
Who killed him? How did he come into my hands?

CADMUS:
Truth is horrible; it always comes at the wrong time.

AGAVÊ:
Tell me. What will it be? My heart is pounding.

CADMUS:
You killed him, you and your sisters.

AGAVÊ:
Where did he die? At home? What kind of place?   *1290*

CADMUS:
The place where—before this—dogs tore Actaeon apart.

AGAVÊ:
But why did he come to Kithairôn? Were the gods against
    him?

CADMUS:
He went to jeer at the god, and at your Bacchic dances too.

AGAVÊ:
What about us—how did we come to land up there?

CADMUS:
You were mad. The whole city had gone into Bacchic frenzy.   *1295*

AGAVÊ:
Dionysus destroyed us. Now I understand.

CADMUS:
He was insulted outrageously when you did not believe he
    was a god.

AGAVÊ:
And my son's body, that I loved so much. Where is it, Father?

1291: Actaeon—the son of Autonoê. See lines 337 and following.

CADMUS:
I brought it here, after a long search. It was hard to find.

AGAVÊ:
1300   Has he been fitted together decently?

> (*Here there is a gap in the only surviving manuscript for this
> part of the play. We must imagine the scene: Cadmus or the
> chorus answers, "No," and Agavê restores the head to the
> body, mourning for her son as she hugs each limb. See the
> Appendix on the play's lost speeches.*)

AGAVÊ:
And Pentheus—did he have any part in my mindless folly?

CADMUS:
He *did* turn out like you—with no reverence for the god.
And so he tied everyone together in one injury [to the god]—
you women, and himself. As a result, he ruined my house
1305   and me. You know I have no male children, and now
I see this offshoot of your womb, poor woman,
dying the worst death possible, the most shameful.

— at hands of women
— mother
— still living

(*To the corpse*)

In you, Child, our home found its eyes.
You held my family together, as the son of my daughter,
1310   and you were a terror to the city. No one wished
to insult the old man, once he saw your face,
because you made them pay a fair penalty.
Now I'll lose my rights, I'll be cast out of my home
—Cadmus the Great, who sowed the race of Thebans
1315   and brought a splendid crop to harvest.
Oh dearest of men—even though you are
no more, I count you, Child, among the friends I love—
never again will you caress my beard,
embrace me, call me "Mother's father,"
1320   ask, "Has anyone done you wrong, old man?
Dishonored or disturbed your heart? Caused you pain?
Tell me, and I'll punish the man who wrongs you, Father."
Now I am miserable and you are wretched,
your mother's pitiful, and her sisters are wretched too.
1325   If there is anyone who despises the divine,

he should look at this man's death and believe in gods.

CHORUS:
 I feel for you, Cadmus. But that grandson of yours
 deserved his punishment, painful as it is for you.

AGAVÊ:
 My life's turned upside down, Father, as you see . . .

> *(Here again a passage has dropped out of the manuscript. We
> must imagine that Agavê offers to help her father as they go
> into exile together. She is interrupted by Dionysus, who makes
> his appearance as a god for the first time in the play, high
> above the royal house. His speech ends with prophecies for each
> of the principal characters. Cadmus is the last to hear his fate.)*

DIONYSUS:
 You, Cadmus, will be transformed into a serpent, while your
   wife   1330
 will turn into a wild animal, changed to the form of snake—
 Harmonia, daughter of Ares, whom you took as wife, though
   you
 were mortal. The oracle of Zeus says that you will drive
 an oxcart, you and your wife, at the head of a troop of
   foreigners.
 You will take and sack many cities with an enormous army,   1335
 but when they plunder the shrine and oracle of Apollo,
 they will cause themselves to have a miserable return
 journey. You and Harmonia, however, will be rescued by
   Ares,
 and he will settle you to live in the Land of the Blessed.
 I pronounce this fate as Dionysus, born of no mortal father,   1340
 for I am the son of Zeus.
 If you had known how to keep your minds
 sound—which you did not wish to do—you would have had
 good fortune, and the son of Zeus would have been your ally.

CADMUS:
 Dionysus, hear our prayer. We have done wrong.

DIONYSUS:
 You learned too late. When you should have known us you
   did not.   1345

CADMUS:
We know that now. But you are too severe in prosecuting us.

DIONYSUS:
I am a god, and you committed an outrage against me.

CADMUS:
Anger does not become a god. You should not be like a
human being.

DIONYSUS:
Zeus, my father, agreed to all this long ago.

AGAVÊ:

(with a cry of despair)

It is a decree, then. Old man, we are banished. How
1350   miserable!

DIONYSUS:
Why put it off? It will be, by necessity.

(Dionysus probably exits on this line.)

CADMUS:
My child, what terrible misery we all face—you, your sisters,
and me. I will arrive as a stranger in a foreign land,
1355   —me an old man. Worse than that, the god has
fated me to lead a ragtag army of foreigners against Greece.
I and my wife Harmonia, daughter of Ares,
will come in the form of wild serpents
at the head of a troop of spearmen
1360   against the tombs and altars of Greece.
And I will have no relief from evil and misery,
no voyage down the Acheron to be at peace below.

AGAVÊ:

(embracing him)

1362: The Acheron was one of the rivers of the underworld. Cadmus does
not mention here his destination in the Land of the Blessed, probably
because endless life seems no consolation to him (Dodds).

Oh, Father, I'll be bereft of you in my exile.

CADMUS:
Why are you wrapping your arms around me
like a swan with its white-haired useless parent?   1365

AGAVÊ:
But where can I turn, when I'm an outcast from my country?

CADMUS:
I don't know, Child. I'm not much help.

AGAVÊ:
Farewell my house, farewell my native land.
I am leaving you now. So unlucky,
my marriage undone. An exile.   1370

CADMUS:
My child, you should go where Aristaeus . . .

AGAVÊ:
I weep for you, Father.

CADMUS:
And I for you, my child, and for your sisters.

AGAVÊ:
It's terrible how
lord Dionysus brought   1375
this calamity on your house.

CADMUS:
Because it was terrible what you did to him;
he had no honor to his name in Thebes.

AGAVÊ:
Farewell, Father.

1371: "Where Aristaeus . . . ": Probably Mt. Kithairôn, where Actaeon, the son of Aristaeus and Agavê's sister Autonoê, was torn apart by his own dogs. The idea would be that she may meet with her sisters there and share the journey into exile. The text breaks off here, but this is probably Cadmus' meaning. Alternatively, Cadmus may be advising his daughters to seek the protection of Aristaeus.

CADMUS:
> Fare *well*, sad Daughter,
1380 though that will be hard where you are going.

AGAVÊ:
> Friends, take me where I can find my sisters
> so that we may be exiles together.

> I'd like to go far away from the curse of Kithairôn,
1385 where I can't see Kithairôn
> where there's no display of a thyrsus to remind me.
> Leave that to other worshipers of Bacchus.

CHORUS:
> Many are the shapes the gods will take,
> many the surprises they perform.
1390 What was thought likely did not transpire,
> and what was unlikely the god made easy.
> That is how this matter ended.

END

Appendix: The Lost Speeches

Of the two surviving manuscripts for the *Bacchae,* one breaks off after line 755, and the other—our only manuscript source for the second half—is missing at least one large section, and probably two, with the result that we do not have Agavê's lament or the beginning of Dionysus' prophecy.

Editors lack consensus as to whether the lament of Agavê came in the gap after line 1300 or the gap after line 1329. Wilamowitz, Murray, and Dodds support the later position and are followed in English reconstructions by Arrowsmith, Williams, and Bagg. Kirk, Seaford, and Leinieks place the lament after 1300, using arguments laid out by C. Robert, making what in my view is a better case. The arguments turn mainly on what makes the best sense in context.

We have three kinds of information for the lost speeches: ancient summaries, fragments, and ancient or medieval texts that imitated the *Bacchae.* Reconstructions of the lost speeches are to be found, for example, in Roux, Leinieks, and Esposito.[1]

---

1. Willink's article on the text of the *Bacchae* is helpful on both the papyrus and the Byzantine imitation.

1. Ancient Summaries

a. The Hypothesis

The ancient summary known as the hypothesis does not mention the lament, but does report on the prophecy: "Dionysus appeared and made an announcement to all. He then made clear what would happen to each one in actual fact, so that no outsider would despise him as human on the basis of mere words."

b. Apsines

Writing in the third century about how to arouse pity, the rhetorician Apsines mentions the missing lament twice:

> Agavê, after recovering from her madness and recognizing that her own child has been torn to pieces, accuses herself, and so arouses pity (9.587).

> By this device, Euripides consciously arouses pity for Pentheus: Holding each of his limbs in her hands, his mother laments in accordance with each of them [the limbs] (9.590).

2. Fragments

a. From an ancient footnote to Aristophanes

For if I had not taken this personal defilement into my hands. . .
(Fr. 847 Nauck, scholion to *Plut.* 907)

b. From Papyri

Two fragments contain enough material to be useful, and missing bits have been filled in speculatively by, for example, Dodds (pp. 243–44). The two fragments are separated by thirty lines that are lost on the papyrus. Both must fall into the same gap in the *Bacchae*, probably the second of the two. What follows is a translation with Dodds's highly speculative supplements:

2a (Probably Cadmus)

. . . bringing Pentheus' furrowed and blood-fouled
limbs, you can be sure, with careful trouble.
Let any mortal who sees this learn the lesson:
It was Zeus who fathered Dionysus the god.

2b (Probably Dionysus)

He whose miserable corpse you hold in your
arms, Agavê, Pentheus, wished to set himself
against your frenzies. But them . . .

. . . his irreverence . . .

3. Imitations

a. From *Christus Patiens*

Probably sometime between the ninth and thirteenth centuries, a
Byzantine writer ("Pseudo-Gregorius") composed a play about
the passion of Christ on the framework of the *Bacchae*. The author
had a complete copy of Euripides' play in front of him and plundered it freely, adapting the lines to suit his purposes. Here is a
fairly straight translation of the lines printed in Diggle's edition of
Euripides. Line numbers refer to the *Christus Patiens*. Scholars
agree that much of this material—though certainly not every
word—was taken from the *Bacchae*. The words bracketed, following Diggle, are probably not from Euripides.

Agavê (probably fits in the gap after *Bacchae* 1300):

I, a miserable wretch who was once [blessed] . . .[2]   *1011*

They did not think to put you in a grave.   *1120*
How did [I bring you down from the tree?]
In what burial mound [may I put] your body?
With what robes [shall I cover] your corpse?

. . . so that [I may draw out] a whole song,   *1256*
kissing the flesh that I nourished.

How may I, with proper care, take him   *1312*
to my breast? In what way shall I mourn?

---

2. Dodds proposes "exultant" to replace the last word.

1449   A little consolation for the dead . . .

1466   Come old man, let us fit the head of this
        [thrice-unlucky man] correctly, and put his whole
        body in tune, as accurately as possible.
        Your dearest face, your young cheeks,
1470   look, with this covering I hide [your head].
        And your blood-fouled and furrowed limbs
        [and parts]—I [cover] them with new robes.

Dionysus (for the gap after *Bacchae* 1329):
        You have learned, since you have paid the penalty you
300   deserved . . .

1360   They were not decent words [the crowd] used
        when they said falsely I was born of someone human.
        I could not bear merely to suffer these insults.

1663   And so he dies at the hands of those who should least
        have killed him, [and he was put in chains and mocked.]
1665   Such were the things done him by a people [who had
        formerly loved him] as a benefactor, now inflamed with malice.
        And he suffered these things not [unwillingly],
        but what the people[3] must suffer—those evils I'll reveal.
        They must leave the city and go among foreigners,
1670   willing or [unwilling], be enslaved, and lose their rights,

        For that is god's decree: [to run] through every foreign land
        to be captives of the spear and suffer many evils.
        [The father of all proclaims to all unbelievers:]
        they are to leave this city in order to pay the penalty
1675   of their unholy pollution to him they killed in their malice,
        never again [to see] their homeland. For it is not holy
        [that murderers should remain by the tombs of the dead.]
        They will come to many cities, [dragging]

---

3. In its late Christian context, this appears to refer to the expulsion of
Jews from their homeland by the Romans. We should not conclude, however, that Dionysus means to expel all Thebans from their land, because it
is plainly his purpose to establish his religion among them at Thebes, and
because his anger is directed specifically at the royal family, and, in this
passage at line 1673, to women.

the yoke of slavery in their misfortune.

As for this man, I will declare the sorrowful destiny he will
    fulfill. *1690*

(Addressed to a woman) As murderer, you must leave the city. *1756*

b. From Seneca's *Phaedra*

Leinieks, alone among editors, uses the following lines from Seneca's Latin play for his reconstruction of the lament: 1247–50,
1254–70, and 1273 of the *Phaedra* (also known as the *Hippolytus*).
As Theseus laments over the battered body of his son Hippolytus,
he tries (and fails) to put pieces of the body back in their proper
places. Leinieks takes these lines to be a version of Agavê's
lament.

I doubt that the lines that follow are based closely on the *Bacchae*. We do not have firm evidence that Agavê did try to reconstruct the body of Pentheus, beyond restoring its head. Further-
more, I do not believe it was Seneca's practice to follow the Greek
word for word. Finally, modern critics have considered the scene
to be an overblown horror show, devised for the taste of Romans
in the bloodthirsty age of Claudius and Nero. Line 1267 is "argu-
ably the worst line in Senecan drama."[4] Readers will see that this
line has competition from others in the vicinity, but should keep in
mind that modern taste is no measure of what ancient audiences
would have admired.

Bring here, bring here the remains of the dear body
and put down the burden of his limbs, collected at random.
Is this Hippolytus? I acknowledge my fault:
I took your life. *1247–50*

Embrace his limbs, whatever remains of your son,
wretched man, lean over them and warm them with your
    breast. *1255*
As his father, put the scattered parts of his torn body
in order and restore each straying part

---

4. Michael Coffey and Roland Mayer, *Seneca Phaedra* (Cambridge: Cambridge University Press, 1990) p. 18, p. 195.

to its place. Here is where his strong right hand should go
here's where to put his left, that knew how to control
1260   the reins. I recognize features of his left side.
But how much is missing still, that I cannot mourn!
Be strong, trembling hands, for their sad work,
and cheeks, you must be dry and hold your tears,
while a father counts out the pieces of his son
1265   and prepares the corpse. What is this that has no shape,
an ugly thing torn on every side with many wounds?
What part it is of yours I do not know, but it is part of you.
Here, put it here. That's not its proper place, but it is empty.
Is this that face that shone with the fire of stars,
1270   and made enemies avert their eyes? Has beauty sunk so far?

1273   Look, take these. They are your father's last gifts.

Notes on Lines and Scenes

The following notes deal briefly with the most important matters of scholarship or interpretation. Readers who wish to go further should consult the commentaries of Dodds and Seaford on each passage, or the notes in Esposito. A citation of Dodds or Seaford in what follows refers to that commentary on the passage in question.

Prologue (1–63): The god announces himself to the audience. His tone is calm, almost pedantic. There is little in the speech to make an audience hate this god or love him, though his anger at the women of his mother's family is evident.

> *Line 1,* Dionysus appears in the role of a human being, a foreign male leader of a troop of Bacchic women. Such troops were not led by men in actual cult practice; instead they felt the presence of the god as their leader.

> *Line 53,* "I'll lead my Maenads like an army": In an early version of the story Pentheus goes to battle against the Maenads.

Entry-song (Parodos, 64–169): The choral entry-song is a cult song in the form of a dithyramb (Seaford). It presents the worship of Dionysus in attractive terms, and the heart-felt devotion of the chorus is unmistakable. We should, however, be conscious of violent elements that might seem to strike a note of discord, as Winnington-Ingram warns us (1939, pp. 31–39).

Line 71, "age-old hymn": So most scholars, reading "always" with "established." But Seaford reads "I will always hymn Dionysus with songs that have been established," and Esposito agrees.

Line 108, The vine in this case is probably bryony, a perennial of the gourd family with no equivalent widely known in North America.

Line 113, "locks of white / lamb's wool": The text is not clear how this is worn; and scholars are not sure how to visualize the wool.

Lines 114–15, "And round your rebel stalks / weave holiness": The chorus strangely puts *hubristas* ("insulting," modifying "stalks") next to the imperative "make holy," suggesting that the stalks (large woody stems of fennel) threaten some danger that is cancelled by the holy purpose to which they are put.

Line 115, "for now the Thunderer leads our revels": Many translations follow Murray in reading a text that gives this meaning instead: "Whoever leads the dance is—i.e., becomes—Bacchus." I follow the more likely reading adopted by Dodds and most recent editors, which means that the god himself is seen as the leader of the dance. In the context of this play, however, we must keep in mind the ambiguity between the male celebrant (whom the god impersonates) and the god himself. See, for example, lines 135 and 145.

Line 135, "He gives delight on mountains": It is unclear whether this is the god delighting the dancers, or the dancer delighting the god. "Probably the god is meant"—Segal 1982, p. 23. If so, then who is it who falls? Segal takes it to be the victim in the hunt, but the syntax requires it to be the god. Perhaps the god is incarnate in the animal. But the passage is probably corrupt (Seaford).

Line 145, "Bacchus": Priest or god? The priest is of course impersonating the god; but here the god has taken the form of the priest. The ambiguity is fitting to the chorus' state of mind.

Line 160, ". . . Phrygian war-cries": Most texts and translations close the quotation two lines further down, but this seems to give a better sense.

Scene One (170–369): The only men who take part in celebrating the new god are two old codgers—the prophet Tiresias and the retired king Cadmus. They prepare to act like Maenads and later argue with Pentheus in defense of the new religion. Men were included in many of the Bacchic rituals, but could not dance with the Maenads. On the two characters, see Introduction, p. xxvii–viii.

The comic elements in this scene do not clash with its religious atmosphere or its larger tragic import. The old men are right to dance for Dionysus; although the sight may be comical, what is really absurd is the reasoning that lies behind their decision to join the party. Old age in itself generally struck ancient Greeks as laughable, and the speech of Tiresias is a marked parody of the New Learning. Euripides could have given Tiresias the voice of sacred authority as a spokesman for Apollo at Delphi, but chose not to do so. On comic elements in the *Bacchae* and their relation to the play as a whole, see Seidensticker (1978), Segal (1982, p. 255), and Halloran (1996). Seaford strongly disagrees (1996, p. 197).

Line 182, Following Dodds I retain this line, although it has been questioned by scholars, including Seaford (who generally minimalizes the humor of the scene).

Line 196, "the rest are mad": On the paradox that sanity requires yielding to Bacchic frenzy, see Introduction, p. xv.

Line 200, "We don't try to be clever with the gods . . .": The text is messy, and the meaning uncertain. Seaford finds it odd that Tiresias condemns sophistry when he is about to launch into a sophistic speech (256–328), but skilled orators frequently disarm their audiences by attacking skill in rhetoric. See, for example, the Mytilenean debate in Thucydides 3.37–51.

Lines 204–5, Recent editors assign these lines to Cadmus, though older editions treated them as part of Tiresias' speech, with this meaning, "*Let* them say I ought to be ashamed, old man that I am, / to take up dancing now, with ivy on my head!"

Lines 208–9, "He'll not exclude anyone": Some Dionysiac rituals excluded men, but generally the religion broke down all barriers, and even slaves could take part in some rituals. Signs of distinction, such as Cadmus' royal chariot, would be inappropriate in this more than democratic cult (line 192).

Lines 266–328, Speech of Tiresias: This is a parody of the style of speaking encomia (praise-speeches) taught by some sophists. Compare it to the speech of Agathon in praise of love in Plato's *Symposium.* Such encomia attribute fine qualities indiscriminately to their subjects; hence Tiresias loads onto Dionysus attributes that rightly belong to Apollo and other gods. Note also his use of the wet/dry antithesis (which bears a whiff of the new science) and the wordplays (which are associated with rhetoric).

Line 293a, The text is messy. Some editors suppose a line has dropped out with the meaning I have supplied here. For another solution with similar meaning, see Seaford.

Line 316, Most editors omit this line as an interpolation.

Line 346, "I will punish him": Pentheus is as violent in his reaction to supposed affronts as is his cousin Dionysus. The speech shows that he, no less than the Maenads on the mountain, is "at the mercy of irrational impulses" (Winnington-Ingram, p. 58).

First Chorus (370–432): Like the Entry-song, this has the form and tone of a cult song.

Line 395, "It's not wise / to lift our thoughts too high": This famous couplet, *to sophon d'ou sophia / to te mê sophon phronein,* uses a play on the two main senses of *sophos*—wise, clever—and contrasts two uses of intelligence. "It's not wise to be a

wiseass, or to think oneself beyond the level of a mortal." See
Introduction, p. xxxix.

Line 427, The text leaves some doubt whether the person who
"steers clear from men who stand out above others" is
Dionysus or the human being he would cherish (as opposed
to the one he hates). The latter seems more likely.

Scene Two (433–518): The rapid-fire dialogue of Pentheus' inter-
rogation of Dionysus is in a form known as *stichomythia,* ideal for
confrontations. Each speech is a full line of iambic verse. Dionysus
answers ambiguously. Pentheus assumes that his methods are
sophistic, but the audience surely knew that deceptive ambiguity
is a proper refuge for a god in contact with someone who is not
initiated.

Line 493, "Let's start by shearing off your pretty goldilocks":
Pentheus probably does not try to cut the hair on stage. The
conventions of Greek theater generally put actions of this sort
offstage.

Second Chorus (519–75): This is mainly in the form of a cult song
calling for the presence of the god. The chorus now sees Pentheus
the way his mother is soon to see him in her frenzy—as a wild
animal.

Scene Three (576–861): The turning point in the play, with the
announcement of a divine presence by means of lightning,
thunder, and earthquake, the messenger's vivid description of
Maenads on the mountain, and the startling change in Pentheus
wrought, apparently, by persuasion.

Lines 576–603, The palace miracles: On the religious signifi-
cance of the scene, Seaford's work is essential reading (1966,
p. 195 ff.). On staging: we cannot be certain, but the majority
of scholars believe that nothing miraculous was visible on
stage. See Dodds (1960, pp. 148–49), Fisher (1992), Seaford
(1996, p. 198).

Lines 604–41, Dionysus' narrative: The meter is the oldest
used in tragic plays, trochaic tetrameter. It is light and fast,

appropriately for an account of "swift and violent action" (Dodds). The series of events is similar to what would happen to Pentheus if he were undergoing initiation (Seaford).

Line 630, "he formed an image of me in the courtyard for Pentheus to attack": Here I follow Diggle, who accepts an emended text (*phasma* for *phôs*). The manuscript reading would have Pentheus chase a light. Seaford, Esposito, and Leinieks accept this, on the grounds that people take a light to be the god during initiation; but Pentheus is chasing someone he thinks is a man.

Line 652, "—that good deed, for which you held Dionysus to blame": Most editors assign this to Pentheus and believe a line is missing after 652. If so, line 652 would be "You call this a 'good deed' of Dionysus? You've slandered him." Then editors insert a line for Dionysus to say something like this: "Ask him yourself. He who set me free is still in Thebes" (line 652*a*, after Kirk). I follow Seaford and Leinieks in accepting the mss, and Leinieks in assigning both lines 651 and 652 to Dionysus. This gives a good sense, although it breaks the rhythm of the scene (as does any solution following the mss).

Lines 664–774, Messenger's speech: More narrator than messenger, he is aware of the story so far (685–87). He emphasizes the orderliness of the Bacchae before they become aware of an intrusion by men (686, 693, 695, 723). Pentheus is exactly wrong: it is only when men interfere that the Bacchae are dangerous.

Lines 756–57, "not bronze, not iron": Diggle and some other editors believe this is interpolated by a copyist from a line now missing, which should have come after line 761 ("the men could not draw blood with their javelins"); the same editors delete "to the black earth" altogether. But the ms reading is not seriously troublesome.

Lines 788–846, Persuasion of Pentheus: Does the god use rhetoric or magic? Probably rhetoric, because line 849 ff. implies that Pentheus is still sane at the end of the scene. Like any expert in persuasion, Dionysus plays on Pentheus' desires both conscious and unconscious. Because he is speaking to an ambitious young soldier, he cleverly casts the operation in a military light, playing on the ambiguity of *stolê* ("outfit" in the sense of a woman's dress, but also in the sense of equipment for an expedition).

Line 810, "Wait": This translates Greek "A," an exclamation that does not fit into the metrical scheme, and probably here expresses protest.

Line 861, "bringing / terrors for initiation, and to the people, gentle grace": My translation reflects one interpretation of a difficult passage (Seaford). Outside of initiation experience, which must be frightening, Dionysus is a kindly god. The alternative reading, as translated by Kirk, is "as a god in perfect essence / most terrible to men, but also most gentle."

Third Chorus (862–911): "To dance the long night!": Among the most beautiful poems in Greek, delicate and yet charged with a cry for justice. This translator does not hear the note of vengeance about which Winnington-Ingram complains (1947, p. 22).

Lines 877–81 and 897–901, Refrain: The meaning of this is disputed. Some early versions take the answer to be the traditional Greek secular principle: the finest gift from the gods is putting down your enemies. But most recent scholars believe that the chorus is putting vengeance into question on religious grounds. On this view, the last line implies a negative answer, which I have supplied in brackets, for the sake of clarity (Seaford, Esposito, Leinieks). Probably the audience knows what Dionysus-worship promises: the only source of joy that cannot be taken away by time and change is initiation, the Dionysiac equivalent of "treasures in heaven" (cf. 73 ff.). (If this is the message, Dionysus himself seems to have missed it; but in other traditions too, gentle deities have been thought to be ruthless with unbelievers.)

Nussbaum and Williams take the refrain to be ambiguous on the point (1990, p. xiii).

Lines 891–92, "No one should ever be above the law, neither in thought nor action": The chorus is attacking those who violate law and custom, but at the same time it is critical of innovation, here as at 895–96. Greeks of this period do not distinguish clearly between "law" and "custom."

Lines 895–96, "power lies . . . with whatever law stands firm in time / by nature ever-natural": The chorus treats traditional law as natural, refusing to consider the sophistic claim that nature is superior to traditional law—an idea that was exploited by reformers of the period who appealed to natural principles as a basis for making changes in law. The chorus rejects such appeals, either on my interpretation of the passage (which follows Seaford) or the alternative one, that long usage makes a law natural (Dodds, Winnington-Ingram). See Introduction, p. xx.

Why do the bringers of a new religion rail against innovation in law or custom? Winnington-Ingram suggests this is because the laws they honor are in fact the natural laws of "impulsive, irrational conduct" (1947, p. 112). But that explanation is not true to the chorus, which consistently sets a high value on quiet wisdom and soundmindedness (sôphrosunê). They appeal to traditional law because what they care about in Dionysus-worship is not its newness—it was, in fact, a very old religion—but the passivity and acceptance it requires of its votaries.

Scene Four (912–76): Dionysus outfits Pentheus for his mission. Cross-dressing is often comical, and there is plainly a note of comedy here, but it is almost drowned out by somber foreshadowing of the sacrifice and death of Pentheus. Sacrificial victims are decked out with similar care; initiation ritual partially mimics sacrifice and in any case may involve cross-dressing. Pentheus is also being readied for the grave; initiates of mystery cults such as that of Dionysus are buried, after death, in linen. They may carry a thyrsus as additional protection.

Line 918, "seeing double": Seaford suggests the effect is due to the mirror used at a stage of initiation.

Line 975, "I am bringing the boy for a great contest . . .": What ensues hardly seems like a contest, so unequal are the powers of the two cousins. But Euripides tends to build his plays around contests (Kirk 1979, p. 16).

Fourth Chorus (977–1023): "Run, swift hounds of madness . . .": Here the devotional beauty of the earlier choral odes is replaced by a passion for justice.

> *Lines 1002–05,* The text is in such bad condition that any translation is speculative. Mine is in line with the thinking of most editors except Leinieks.

> *Line 1005,* "Wisdom you may have": The chorus has no wish to be wise in the sense of clever; there is a quieter wisdom, however, which they cherish. See lines 395 and 1150; also Introduction, p. xxvi.

> *Lines 1017–18,* "Be seen as a bull, be seen many-headed, / be seen as a serpent, or lion blazing fire": These are visible forms Dionysus takes, and this may be a standard prayer calling for an epiphany of the god—an event in which the god shows himself to mortals in all his power.

Scene Five (1024–1152): The second messenger brings the news that is at the heart of the play, but he does not fit well into the drama on stage or off. We are given no reason why he should want to deliver this long story to a bevy of foreign women at whom he is angry, and he seems to be more an omniscient narrator than a participant on the mountain, since he sees what Pentheus evidently does not (lines 1053–62—unless Pentheus means only that he cannot see what he expected to see).

As in Scene Three, the Maenads become what men fear only when they are disturbed by men. And what is it men fear? Pentheus says it is sex (which he would actually find titillating). But the men on the mountain are terrified not by watching women engaged in sex, but by seeing women magically empowered to do what men should do at their most manly: In the earlier scene, the Maenads swept down upon farming hamlets like an enemy army; now, in this scene, they take on the male role of hunters.

> *Line 1060,* "those phony Maenads": Here I follow the manuscript, as do Esposito and most others. Seaford, following

Jackson, reads "those diseased Maenads."

Lines 1066–67, "like a round wheel / when the compass
scribes its running arc": A craftsman fixes a peg to the center
of a large board, runs a string from the peg to a sharp instrument, and scribes a line around the outline of the wheel before cutting it out. Imagine Dionysus pulling the tree from the
top with his right hand while rounding the trunk into an arc
with his left, so that it does not simply snap off. (Some editors
have thought that the metaphor refers to a lathe; but wheels
are too large for turning on a lathe.)

The death of Pentheus follows in many details the pattern set
for sacrifice and initiation. The stoning of the victim is especially significant. See Seaford's note on the passage and his
discussion (1994, pp. 289–90, 314–17).

Lines 1091–92: Omitted as spurious, following Dodds, Seaford, and other editors.

Line 1104, "But those were no iron crowbars, and their efforts
led nowhere": These women hunters, unlike men, do better
without tools (see lines 1173, 1205–7).

Line 1150, "have a sound mind and reverence for / whatever
belongs to gods": The virtues of *sôphrosunê* (modesty, soundmindedness, self-control) and *eusebeia* (reverence, piety) in-
voked here have been praised frequently by the chorus and
here seem to be given as the answer to the question they
asked at lines 877–81 ("What is wise, what is the finest gift /
that gods can give to mortals?"). The audience may be supposed to feel irony here, now that they have heard how vio-
lently Maenads can lose control of themselves: "Here [i.e., "in
the full horror of their revenge"] is the sanity, the piety, the
honour and wisdom of Bacchanals" (Winnington-Ingram
1939, p. 133). But the audience, with its own experience of
Dionysus-worship, surely knew better: this is what happens
when Dionysus is denied, not in civilized Athens, but in brutal Thebes, and not to ordinary people, but to those who tried
to be the first family of Thebes.

Line 1151, "the most wise of all pursuits a human being can follow": Here I follow the manuscript. Seaford and Esposito, following a fifth-century quotation, read a text that yields: "the wisest *possession* for mortals to use."

Fifth Chorus (1153–64) and Exodos (Final Scene 1165–1392): Agavê's entrance blends smoothly into the chorus's brief triumph song, as she is assimilated into their rhythms and their dance. The opening of the last scene is in lyric meter, and has an antiphonal structure. When the chorus asks Agavê to display her kill, however, the verse returns to the standard iambic meter of speech and dialogue.

Winnington-Ingram complains that the vengeance of Dionysus is indiscriminate (p. 142), but, as Seaford points out, only the royal family is destroyed. As far as we can tell, the rest of Thebes lives on undisturbed to enjoy the pleasures, relaxations, and possible dangers of Dionysus-worship; indeed, they are probably relieved to be free of a king who terrorizes them (line 1310). Even the royal family suffers in different degrees—Pentheus least, because he dies (and, though he does not know it, his death serves, as a soldier's would, to save the city from peril). Agavê suffers most, because she and her surviving sisters committed the outrage against Dionysus that turned him against Thebes—they disbelieved their own sister about her pregnancy. See below, on lines 1344–48.

Our only ms is in especially bad shape at the end of the play, and there are probably two major gaps. (Certainly there is a gap after line 1329, and probably after line 1300 as well.) One substantial speech has been lost entirely and another cut short. The lost speech is Agavê's lament, although we have some evidence as to its content. It probably dropped out after line 1300, but some scholars would place it in the gap after 1329. We have lost the beginning of Dionysus' proclamation and prophecy, having only the astounding future he gives to Cadmus.

I cannot reconstruct the lost speeches with the confidence I have had in replacing the odd lines missing throughout the play. Many translators have attempted reconstructions, and C. K. Williams has achieved literary elegance in his. For translations of the evidence concerning these gaps, see the Appendix.

Line 1158, "the staff / that promises Hades": On the evidence that the thyrsus was associated with journeys to the underworld see Seaford's note.

Line 1166, "What are you shouting about?": Text uncertain. Following Seaford.

Line 1175, "A lion's cub": At least one word is missing from the manuscript. Following most editors, I have supplied "lion's."

Lines 1185–87, The image of the young bull: In Dionysiac frenzy, Agavê now sees her son as a young sacrificial bull. So do most editors; but the word usually translated "young bull" can also mean a shoot or twig, and Leinieks takes it in this sense, so that Agavê sees Pentheus' hair as grape tendrils from a sprig of vine on her thyrsus, hanging below the chin of the lion.

Line 1196, "outstanding": See the chorus's condemnation of people who do not avoid what is outstanding, at line 429.

Line 1216, Enter Cadmus: The old man's experience on the mountain seems to have changed him. Although he was virtually senile at his first appearance, he now speaks like a man at the height of his mental powers.

Lines 1244–45, Seaford would omit these lines as spurious.

Line 1329, The epiphany of Dionysus, probably *ex machina* (elevated), occurred during the gap in our play. Because we do not know what he said before turning to specific prophecies, we should be slow to agree with Winnington-Ingram that the event is "spectacular but empty" (p. 144).

Lines 1344–48, Because of the gap, we cannot be certain who it is that talks back to Dionysus, but most recent editors have chosen to assign all of the lines to Cadmus. It is hard to believe that Agavê would be capable of such a response at this point. The assignment to Cadmus is appropriate in any case because only he, of those present, can complain that he has suffered unjustly. He had, after all, made a sanctuary of Semélê's tomb. We should keep in mind, however, that Cadmus' observance of Dionysus-worship was due not to sincere belief but to family-feeling, and that although Dionysus praised him for fencing off a sanctuary at his birthplace, it is not the act of a Dionysiac to declare a place off limits.

Line 1351, Probable exit of Dionysus. He may have been followed by his troop of Maenads, the chorus.

Line 1368, Here the meter changes back to lyric form, and the musical accompaniment probably resumed.

Lines 1377–78, If the manuscript is right, this speech belongs to Dionysus: "It is terrible what I suffered from you . . ." Most scholars, however, accept the emended version as translated here.

Lines 1388–92, The exit lines of the chorus: the same or similar lines are found at the end of the *Alcestis, Andromache, Helen,* and *Medea.* Some scholars consider them an actor's interpolation. Dodds would retain them, but Seaford would not.